W9-AEH-219

OPPOSING
VIEWPOINTS®
SERIES

Energy Alternatives

Other Books of Related Interest:

Opposing Viewpoints Series

The Environment

Offshore Drilling

Renewable Energy

At Issue Series

The Alaskan Natural Gas Pipeline

The Energy Crisis

What Is the Impact of E-Waste?

Current Controversies Series

Conserving the Environment

The Green Movement

"Congress shall make no law . . . abridging the freedom of speech, or of the press."

First Amendment to the U.S. Constitution

The basic foundation of our democracy is the First Amendment guarantee of freedom of expression. The Opposing Viewpoints Series is dedicated to the concept of this basic freedom and the idea that it is more important to practice it than to enshrine it.

OPPOSING VIEWPOINTS® SERIES

Energy Alternatives

David Haugen, Susan Musser, and Vickey Kalambakal,
Book Editors

GREENHAVEN PRESS
A part of Gale, Cengage Learning

GALE
CENGAGE Learning™

Detroit • New York • San Francisco • New Haven, Conn • Waterville, Maine • London

Christine Nasso, *Publisher*
Elizabeth Des Chenes, *Managing Editor*

© 2010 Greenhaven Press, a part of Gale, Cengage Learning

Gale and Greenhaven Press are registered trademarks used herein under license.

For more information, contact:
Greenhaven Press
27500 Drake Rd.
Farmington Hills, MI 48331-3535
Or you can visit our Internet site at gale.cengage.com

For product information and technology assistance, contact us at

Gale Customer Support, 1-800-877-4253
For permission to use material from this text or product, submit all requests online at www.cengage.com/permissions

Further permissions questions can be emailed to permissionrequest@cengage.com

Articles in Greenhaven Press anthologies are often edited for length to meet page requirements. In addition, original titles of these works are changed to clearly present the main thesis and to explicitly indicate the author's opinion. Every effort is made to ensure that Greenhaven Press accurately reflects the original intent of the authors. Every effort has been made to trace the owners of copyrighted material.

Cover image copyright Gino Caron, 2010. Used under license from Shutterstock.com.

LIBRARY OF CONGRESS CATALOGING-IN-PUBLICATION DATA

Energy alternatives / David Haugen, Susan Musser, and Vickey Kalambakal, book editors.
  p. cm. -- (Opposing viewpoints)
  Includes bibliographical references and index.
  ISBN 978-0-7377-4962-5 (hbk.) -- ISBN 978-0-7377-4963-2 (pbk.)
  1. Renewable energy resources--Juvenile literature. 2. Renewable energy resources--United States--Juvenile literature. I. Haugen, David M., 1969- II. Musser, Susan. III. Kalambakal, Vickey.
  TJ808.2.E64 2010
  333.79'4--dc22

                      2009052253

Printed in the United States of America
1 2 3 4 5 6 7 14 13 12 11 10

Contents

Chapter 3: Should Alternatives to Gasoline-Powered Vehicles Be Pursued?

Chapter 4: What Should Be the Government's Role in Advancing Alternative Energy?

Why Consider Opposing Viewpoints?

> *"The only way in which a human being can make some approach to knowing the whole of a subject is by hearing what can be said about it by persons of every variety of opinion and studying all modes in which it can be looked at by every character of mind. No wise man ever acquired his wisdom in any mode but this."*
>
> *John Stuart Mill*

In our media-intensive culture it is not difficult to find differing opinions. Thousands of newspapers and magazines and dozens of radio and television talk shows resound with differing points of view. The difficulty lies in deciding which opinion to agree with and which "experts" seem the most credible. The more inundated we become with differing opinions and claims, the more essential it is to hone critical reading and thinking skills to evaluate these ideas. Opposing Viewpoints books address this problem directly by presenting stimulating debates that can be used to enhance and teach these skills. The varied opinions contained in each book examine many different aspects of a single issue. While examining these conveniently edited opposing views, readers can develop critical thinking skills such as the ability to compare and contrast authors' credibility, facts, argumentation styles, use of persuasive techniques, and other stylistic tools. In short, the Opposing Viewpoints Series is an ideal way to attain the higher-level thinking and reading skills so essential in a culture of diverse and contradictory opinions.

In addition to providing a tool for critical thinking, Opposing Viewpoints books challenge readers to question their own strongly held opinions and assumptions. Most people form their opinions on the basis of upbringing, peer pressure, and personal, cultural, or professional bias. By reading carefully balanced opposing views, readers must directly confront new ideas as well as the opinions of those with whom they disagree. This is not to simplistically argue that everyone who reads opposing views will—or should—change his or her opinion. Instead, the series enhances readers' understanding of their own views by encouraging confrontation with opposing ideas. Careful examination of others' views can lead to the readers' understanding of the logical inconsistencies in their own opinions, perspective on why they hold an opinion, and the consideration of the possibility that their opinion requires further evaluation.

Evaluating Other Opinions

To ensure that this type of examination occurs, Opposing Viewpoints books present all types of opinions. Prominent spokespeople on different sides of each issue as well as well-known professionals from many disciplines challenge the reader. An additional goal of the series is to provide a forum for other, less known, or even unpopular viewpoints. The opinion of an ordinary person who has had to make the decision to cut off life support from a terminally ill relative, for example, may be just as valuable and provide just as much insight as a medical ethicist's professional opinion. The editors have two additional purposes in including these less known views. One, the editors encourage readers to respect others' opinions—even when not enhanced by professional credibility. It is only by reading or listening to and objectively evaluating others' ideas that one can determine whether they are worthy of consideration. Two, the inclusion of such viewpoints encourages the important critical thinking skill of objectively evaluating an author's credentials and bias. This evaluation will illuminate an author's reasons for taking a particular stance on an issue and will aid in readers' evaluation of the author's ideas.

It is our hope that these books will give readers a deeper understanding of the issues debated and an appreciation of the complexity of even seemingly simple issues when good and honest people disagree. This awareness is particularly important in a democratic society such as ours in which people enter into public debate to determine the common good. Those with whom one disagrees should not be regarded as enemies but rather as people whose views deserve careful examination and may shed light on one's own.

Thomas Jefferson once said that "difference of opinion leads to inquiry, and inquiry to truth." Jefferson, a broadly educated man, argued that "if a nation expects to be ignorant and free . . . it expects what never was and never will be." As individuals and as a nation, it is imperative that we consider the opinions of others and examine them with skill and discernment. The Opposing Viewpoints Series is intended to help readers achieve this goal.

David L. Bender and Bruno Leone,
Founders

Introduction

> "I believe that with the proper amount of research, whether it be public or private, we will have solar roofs that will enable the American family to be able to generate their own electricity. And it's coming. . . . What I'm talking about is a comprehensive approach to solving a national issue, which is dependence on oil, and how best to protect this environment. You know, it's time to get rid of the old, stale debates on the environment and recognize new technologies are going to enable us to achieve a lot of objectives at the same time."
>
> George W. Bush,
> speech given at a national
> renewable energy conference
> in St. Louis, October 12, 2006

> "The possibilities of renewable energy are limitless. . . . We have been talking about energy independence since Americans were waiting in gas lines during the 1970s. . . . But each and every year, we become more, not less, addicted to oil—a 19th-century fossil fuel that is dirty, dwindling, and dangerously expensive."
>
> Barack Obama,
> campaign speech given in Las Vegas,
> June 24, 2008

In 1973 energy policy in the United States shifted from an issue relegated to closed congressional discussions to a highly public concern debated around watercoolers and at dinner tables. In October of that year, the Organization of Arab Petroleum Exporting Countries (OAPEC), which included the Organization of the Petroleum Exporting Countries (OPEC), Egypt, and Syria, commenced an oil embargo against the United States following the country's military support of Israel in the Yom Kippur War. In the months that followed, the price of a gallon of gasoline nearly doubled, and at the end of February 1974, the fuel pumps at one-fifth of the gas stations in the United States were empty. For the first time in U.S. history, average individuals nationwide began to realize the risks associated with the country's dependence on oil.

While energy independence quickly became a driving force in determining the country's future energy policy, a second factor emerged on the public stage and also began to influence the discussion about fossil fuel consumption and the need for alternative energies. The Environmental Protection Agency (EPA), established in 1970, began to push environmental policy to the forefront of government discussion, and climate change became one of the agency's main concerns toward the end of the decade. Scientists showed that the temperature of the earth has been steadily increasing since the 1950s, and most agreed that the increase in temperature had resulted from greenhouse gases emitted through the burning of fossil fuels for energy. Since the 1970s, this revelation—coupled with the problematic reliance on foreign oil—has prompted policy makers and industry leaders to investigate energy alternatives that not only promote energy independence, but also decrease the amount of greenhouse gases poured into the atmosphere through the burning of fossil fuels.

As public concern about the environment and the vulnerability of the country's energy sources has steadily increased over time, politicians have focused much of their campaign rhetoric and policy making on creating a national energy policy to address their constituents' worries. Beginning with Richard Nixon—who was in office during the 1973 oil crisis—all U.S. presidents have vowed to help the country transition to energy independence, and most have at least paid lip service to the environmental consequences of not making the transition via an investment in environmentally friendly alternative energies. The progress of the various administrations' energy policies remains debatable, but few critics believe that the successes attending any legislative action have achieved the ultimate goal. Writing in the journal *Daedalus* in 2006, energy experts Marilyn A. Brown, Benjamin K. Sovacool, and Richard F. Hirsh lament the inability of any U.S. president to pass meaningful legislation to establish a secure, sustainable source of energy. They write, "Despite more than three decades of such efforts [to reduce dependence on foreign oil], the United States has not achieved the goal of energy independence." America now imports 62 percent of the oil it consumes every year compared with 35 percent in 1973. Thus most observers concur that alternative energy sources have yet to make a significant impact on America's energy production.

Because critics have enumerated the shortcomings of policy to date, presidential administrations in the first decade of the twenty-first century have made energy policy a cornerstone of their national agendas. While differing greatly in their specific approaches, former president George W. Bush and current president Barack Obama developed energy plans emphasizing the long-term investment in alternatives to current energy sources such as petroleum, natural gas, and coal while struggling to reduce foreign oil consumption in the short term. As with energy policies of the past, the plans' relative success or failure remains a source of contention in government and society at large.

In his first term as president, George W. Bush believed the best way to cut U.S. dependence on foreign oil was to expand domestic oil production. He advocated drilling in protected wildlife areas such as the Arctic National Wildlife Refuge and in new offshore locations to tap America's native reserves. While this proposal would have curbed foreign oil consumption, it would not have limited the release of greenhouse gases, and it therefore never gained widespread, bipartisan support. As criticism of his proposed plan to drill in protected areas grew, Bush's energy policy quickly shifted toward the implementation of alternative energy sources. In the spring and summer of 2001, the construction of new nuclear power plants and increasing research and development of clean coal power plants signaled the change in direction. Neither of these technologies, however, had great public support. Nuclear power retained its aura of danger, and researchers could not agree that clean coal was really environmentally friendly. Neither could be forsaken, however, for they alone were capable of providing the amount of power the nation required.

During Bush's second term in office, his administration restructured its energy policy once more. While the expansion of nuclear power remained a central goal, the administration placed a more urgent emphasis on clean coal technology and alternative fuels for cars. Throwing support to the FutureGen Initiative in 2006, Bush planned to see the first clean coal power plant—producing energy without the release of pollutants and greenhouse gases—built and operational by 2012. Additionally, the president pledged billions of dollars to the development and use of ethanol—fuel produced from corn or other renewable sources—to fuel the nation's vehicles. The government provided subsidies to farmers to increase corn production, and those building new fuel stations would receive tax credits if they catered to ethanol-powered automotives.

Even while lauding the benefits of alternative energy sources and apparently dedicating more time and money to their development, Bush received criticism from pundits and legislators who charged that the president's actions did not match his promises. Over the course of Bush's remaining years in office, few ethanol stations dotted the nation's highways and clean coal failed to become a reality. Some believed it was because the president was not committing enough resources to the project, given that the lion's share of the national budget was funding wars in Iraq and Afghanistan. In the journal *Nature Biotechnology*, Jeffrey L. Fox reported that the administration's fiscal year 2009 budget appropriated only $1.26 billion, 5 percent of the total Department of Energy budget, to developing and expanding renewable energy sources. Carol Werner, executive director of the Environmental and Energy Study Institute, was quoted in this same article stating, "Funding priorities reflected in the president's FY 2009 budget appear to conflict with the goals of expanding renewable energy development and making the economy more energy efficient."

Some conservative analysts also critiqued the Bush administration's energy policy. Following the president's State of the Union address in 2006, Ben Lieberman of the Heritage Foundation disparaged the president's proposed approaches to energy independence because they depended on too much government involvement. He jibed, "Rather than expand government interference in energy markets and pick winners and losers from among emerging technologies, Washington should get out of the way and let market forces work." By the end of Bush's presidency, both policy analysts and the general public frowned on his inability to bring about the widespread implementation of energy alternatives to achieve energy independence and reduce climate change.

The public's discontent with the Bush administration's energy policy became an opportunity for Barack Obama during the 2008 presidential campaign and in the first year of his presidency to secure goodwill for his national energy program. Obama's plan calls for America's transition to sustainable energy resources to provide the nation's power. In light of the recession that began in 2008, much of the Obama administration's agenda focuses on developing and building an alternative energy economy in the United States. This plan proposes to create jobs for millions of Americans in the design and manufacture of alternative energy technologies such as solar, wind, and geothermal power, and the building of a new, nationwide electricity grid to transport that power. He envisions a system in which renewable energy sources will generate a quarter of the country's power by 2025.

In addition to funding this development with government money, his plan provides incentives for Americans to install these types of energy sources in their businesses and homes. Americans will receive tax credits for installing solar panels and using energy efficient appliances, and those who purchase hybrid vehicles will earn tax breaks. Obama proposed these incentives to achieve the goal of having 1 million American-made, 150-miles-per-gallon, plug-in hybrid cars on the road by 2015.

Even with renewed focus on energy alternatives, many pundits and commentators are skeptical of the costs and supposed benefits of Obama's plan. Daniel Holler, the Senate relations deputy for the Heritage Foundation, disapproves of the Obama administration's drive to convert the country to renewable energy sources. He claims in a May 2009 issue of *Human Events* magazine, "A radical, government-mandated, expensive conversion to renewable resources will create many more problems than it pretends to solve." He worries that Obama's energy policy will recreate the conditions that led to the collapse of the U.S. financial system. Indeed, many people worry that the nation cannot afford to spend lavishly on revamping the nation's infrastructure when millions of Americans are only tenuously holding onto their jobs and their homes.

Other individuals are unsure whether Obama's plan is dedicated enough to the alternative energy sources they believe necessary to foster a successful energy policy. Writing in an April 2009 *New York Times* op-ed column, Thomas Friedman contends that Obama's energy plan does not provide sufficient incentive for individuals to switch to alternative energy sources. Pushing for a tax on carbon emissions as a means of forcing America to convert, he states, "Without a fixed, long-term, durable price on carbon, none of the Obama clean-tech initiatives will achieve the scale needed to have an impact on climate change or make America the leader it must be in the next great industrial revolution: E.T., or energy technology." Friedman advocates a pricing mechanism to ensure that alternative energy technologies are more financially attractive than traditional energy sources.

Because it is still too early to tell whether Obama's energy plan will succeed in promoting energy alternatives to achieve energy independence and mitigate the human impact on climate change, debate is likely to continue. Ultimately, the issue will come to a head either by legislation or by the simple fact that fossil fuels cannot sustain the planet's energy needs indefinitely. The authors of the viewpoints anthologized in *Opposing Viewpoints: Energy Alternatives* recognize this reality. In chapters titled "Are Alternative Energy Sources Necessary?" "What Alternative Energy Sources Should Be Pursued?" "Should Alternatives to Gasoline-Powered Vehicles Be Pursued?" and "What Should Be the Government's Role in Advancing Alternative Energy?" politicians, spokespersons, experts, and analysts offer their views on how the nation should proceed in addressing the growing demand for energy and the least destructive, most efficient and economical means of meeting it. Each chapter examines different types of alternative energies and the feasibility of their implementation. In addition, the commentators take up the moral and environmental issues that surround the utilization of certain alternatives. Thus, this anthology assesses not only how energy alternatives might help the country become energy independent, but also how well they preserve the planet for generations to come.

OPPOSING
VIEWPOINTS®
SERIES

CHAPTER 1

Are Alternative Energy Sources Necessary?

Chapter Preface

Senators Barack Obama and Joe Biden jointly issued the New Energy for America plan as they campaigned to win the White House in 2008. "Our country cannot afford politics as usual," their fact sheet insisted, "not at a moment when the energy challenge we face is so great and the consequences of inaction are so dangerous. We must act quickly and we must act boldly to transform our entire economy—from our cars and our fuels to our factories and our buildings." As part of realizing this goal, the running mates argued that government, industry, and the public must work to "ensure 10 percent of our electricity comes from renewable sources by 2012, and 25 percent by 2025." In 2007, the most recent year providing statistical evidence, the Energy Information Administration (EIA) reported that only 8.5 percent of America's electricity comes from renewable sources such as wind power, solar power, biomass fuel, geothermal energy, and tidal forces. In addition, the EIA predicted that the contribution of renewable sources is likely to rise just 7.3 percent by 2030.

Whether renewable resources can or cannot account for a quarter of America's electricity needs by 2025, experts still debate the capability of the nation to wean itself off its reliance on fossil fuels and achieve Obama's dream of energy independence. Many analysts believe that the world has enough oil in existing supplies to keep the world's gasoline-powered engines humming for a long time. Even the EcoWorld energy news Web site corrected those environmentalists who hue and cry over rapidly dwindling oil stocks by noting that the best estimates suggest that the world will not drain existing supplies for 110 years. Other authorities add that if untapped wells are finally drilled, the amount of recoverable oil increases significantly, and these new reserves combined with the old ones will yield more oil as drilling and extraction techniques improve. The *Wall Street Journal* writes that "even a 10% gain in extraction efficiency on a global scale will unlock 1.2 to 1.6 trillion barrels of extra resources—an additional 50-year supply at current consumption rates."

The outlook on coal, on the other hand, which supplies 22 percent of America's energy needs and over half of its electric power, has changed in recent years. For decades, researchers have assumed that America's coal reserves were so extensive that eventually liquefied coal would replace oil when it dried up. A Caltech scientist, however, proposed a new model in 2008 that showed global coal stocks falling far below previous estimates. The Energy Watch Group in Germany similarly predicted that coal recovery would peak in 2025. If the United States cannot rely on its abundant coal to power the future, then Obama and Biden's faith in renewable energies might have to translate into reality.

In the following chapter, commentators examine the need and the feasibility of moving from a global, carbon-based energy society to one that seeks to achieve independence from fossil fuels. Some, like Obama and Biden, believe change must occur in the lifetime of the present generation or else ecological and economic disaster could result. Others claim that alternative energies—because of their expense, unreliability, and limited energy output—could never supplant oil, coal, and natural gas. Coupled with a reliance on technology and the relative abundance of fossil fuels that remain untapped, these hopeful analysts assume that crisis is far off and that humanity still has time to prepare for change. In a world that assuredly will exhaust its resources, the overriding question is how soon change must come.

> "The remaining areas of doubt about the date of the oil peak are evaporating almost as quickly as those about the severity of climate change."

Peaks in Global Oil Production Rates Are Imminent

David Strahan

In the following viewpoint, David Strahan insists that neither those who warn of climate change nor the general public are sufficiently concerned about peak oil, the point at which the planet's oil reserves will begin to decline. Strahan claims that many countries are experiencing declines in oil production and that the peak in global oil will occur before 2020. He believes that the world is unprepared for weaning itself off oil and should be devising energy strategies to cope with the reality that oil will run out sooner rather than later. Strahan is an award-winning journalist and the author of The Last Oil Shock, *a book that illustrates his predictions about oil depletion.*

David Strahan, "Who's Afraid of Oil Depletion?" *Ecologist*, vol. 37, April 2007, pp. 22–23. This article first appeared on www.theecologist.org in April, 2007. Copyright © 2007 MIT Press Journals. Reproduced by permission.

As you read, consider the following questions:

1. As Strahan claims, what will a 3 percent per year reduction in oil production after 2010 mean for total greenhouse gas emissions over the subsequent twenty-year period?

2. Of the nearly one hundred oil-producing nations in the world, how many does Strahan say are already in terminal decline in oil production?

3. Why does Strahan say that the global fuel alternatives to oil could be more destructive to the climate than the burning of oil?

What is it about climate change campaigners and peak oil—the two words you almost never hear them utter? The idea that global oil production will soon go into terminal decline ought to be a godsend; it makes the kinds of things they have been lobbying for all the more urgent and compelling. Yet most of the big NGOs [nongovernmental organizations] continue studiously to ignore the idea. True, the Soil Association has recently taken to peak oil like an organic duck to water, but searching the Web sites of Greenpeace and Friends of the Earth brings up only a couple of brief and noncommittal references buried deep in reports that few have probably read. Most peak oilers accept global warming without question, but the feeling is evidently not mutual.

They ought to be such natural allies. For every climate argument there's a strong peak one to reinforce it. The climate change campaigner wants to reduce food miles and encourage local agriculture in order to cut carbon emissions; the peak oiler wants the same to secure the food supply when fuel runs short. The climate change campaigner wants higher vehicle fuel economy to cut carbon emissions; the peak oiler to help defer the date of peak production and its attendant economic crisis. Broadly speaking both agendas call for an early and rapid transition away from the oil economy, but peak oil arguments have the advantage of even greater urgency; despite the horrors of the recent IPCC [Intergovernmental Panel on Climate Change] Fourth Assessment Report [AR4], the most devastating impacts of peak will come far sooner than the most catastrophic of climate change—within a decade or so rather than a century. So why are climate change campaigners so wary of enlisting peak arguments?

After Peak Oil, Emissions Still Rise

On both sides of this divide, I get a certain sense of competitive shroud waving: My crisis is bigger than yours. And perhaps peak oilers are as much to blame for this. Many climate change campaigners seem to have got the impression that those who worry predominantly about peak oil must somehow be suggesting that climate change is not such a monumental problem, or even that 'running out' of oil will solve global warming. There may be some naïve peak oilers who actually believe this, but as far as I am aware no serious writer on the subject has advanced such a view. . . . It is perfectly possible to run short of oil and pollute the planet to destruction simultaneously.

The International Energy Agency's [IEA] business-as-usual forecast shows total CO_2 emissions from fossil fuels growing from 26 billion tonnes in 2004 to 40 billion in 2030. The IEA does not accept the case for an early oil peak, but as I show in [Strahan's book] *The Last Oil Shock*, their forecast relies in part on a demonstrably overoptimistic resource assessment. However, if we take . . . [IEA's] forecast and impose an oil peak in 2010, followed immediately by production decline at 3% per year, total emissions still rise by 25% over the next two decades, to 32 billion tonnes. The massive fall in oil-related emissions—the result of oil production slumping 40 million barrels per day—is simply overwhelmed by continuing growth from gas and coal, which are not so immediately resource-constrained. Neither side can now seriously believe oil depletion solves climate change, or that this spurious idea is any reason to resist the persuasive case for an early global oil production peak.

No Doubt About the Peak Oil Date

Perhaps a more reasonable objection of climate change campaigners, until recently at least, is uncertainty about the reliability of the forecasts, and when exactly the peak will arrive. It is perfectly true that previous predictions of a global oil peak have come and gone without the sky falling in, and nobody likes to be accused of crying wolf. When I interviewed Greenpeace director Stephen Tindale for *The Last Oil Shock*, he was ready to accept that peak oil might provide additional ammunition for his organization, but was adamant they should not include it in their armoury. "This is a highly contested area", he argued. "If it turned out that the oil peak thesis was wrong, and we'd been using it, then that would undermine and discredit other things we had been saying". For any organization that has to spend much of its time fighting off climate sceptics [skeptics], such caution is perhaps understandable, but it is no longer justified.

The remaining areas of doubt about the date of the oil peak are evaporating almost as quickly as those about the severity of climate change. Out of just under 100 oil-producing countries worldwide, 60 are already in terminal decline. New countries join the list almost yearly, and since the late 1990s have included significant producers such as Britain, Norway, Denmark, Mexico, Argentina, Colombia, Australia and Oman. In aggregate, OECD [Organisation for Economic Co-operation and Development] oil production has been in decline since 1997, and most forecasters—even including noted optimists such as the IEA and ExxonMobil—now predict that the entire world except for OPEC [Organization of the Petroleum Exporting Countries] will peak by early in the next decade.

From then on, by common consent, the only thing standing between us and the conventional oil peak is the cartel. There are severe doubts about the real scale of OPEC's reserves, and most serious independent observers do not expect its production to stave off the global peak for long.

Despite government denials—the official position in both Britain and America is that there will be no peak before 2030—this notion is now being taken seriously by officials at the highest levels. As I report in *The Last Oil Shock*, the consultancy PFC Energy has briefed [former U.S. vice president] Dick Cheney that on a conservative reserves estimate OPEC oil production—and thus global output—could peak by 2015. In a well-researched speech at Stanford University last year [2006], Sir David Manning, [former British prime minister] Tony Blair's chief foreign policy advisor between 9/11 [2001 terrorist attacks on the United States] and the invasion of Iraq, noted the consensus was narrowing to "some point between 2010 and 2020". At an Energy Institute lunch in 2005, the government's chief scientific advisor Sir David King told me emphatically "ten years or less". And yet still some climate change campaigners remain suspicious to the point of hostility. One well-known author even ludicrously suggested to me recently that peak oil was nothing but oil company propaganda. He was apparently unaware that ExxonMobil is just as contemptuous of peak oil as it has been of climate change.

A World Unprepared for the Disaster to Come

This continuing denial of peak oil is myopic in the extreme, since not only does falling oil production not solve climate change, it also seems likely to make fighting global warming very much harder. When oil production goes into decline, the price of crude [oil] is likely to soar, with devastating economic effect. The kind of long-term impacts attributed by [Nicholas] Stern [the author of *The Stern Review on the Economics of Cli-*

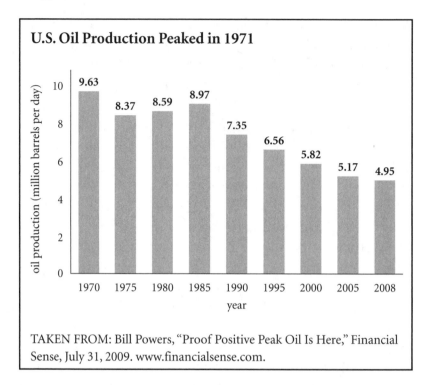

U.S. Oil Production Peaked in 1971

oil production (million barrels per day)

TAKEN FROM: Bill Powers, "Proof Positive Peak Oil Is Here," Financial Sense, July 31, 2009. www.financialsense.com.

mate Change] to climate change could arrive much sooner and in a single thunderclap. With the economy reeling from blows "similar to those associated with the great wars and the economic depression of the first half of the 20th century", where will the money come from to make the massive investments necessary to create the new energy infrastructure? And faced with the likely re-emergence of mass unemployment, will the political priority be to impose a high carbon price, or simply to keep the lights burning at lowest cost?

Peak oil could also sabotage attempts to fight climate change by paradoxically increasing greenhouse gas emissions, if oil depletion forces us to exploit the wrong kinds of fuel. The alternatives to crude oil are all resource constrained and unlikely to fill the gap—at least not in time—but they still have the potential to do enormous climate damage. Burning rain forest and peat lands to create palm oil plantations for biofuels releases vast amounts of CO_2, and has already turned Indonesia into the world's third biggest emitter after America and China. Synthetic transport fuels made from gas using the Fischer-Tropsch chemical process emit even more carbon on a well-to-wheels basis than conventional crude. When the feedstock is coal the emissions double. So in the unlikely scenario that we manage to replace more than half the yawning conventional deficit with coal-based fuel, but not all of it, we would still suffer fuel shortage while emitting even more CO_2 than in the current business-as-usual forecast—the worst of all possible worlds.

Ignoring peak is even more shortsighted in light of climate change campaigners' failure to make significant headway in changing most people's behaviour—even when preaching to the choir. A recent survey of *Guardian* and *Independent* [UK newspapers] readers revealed the gulf between their green self-image and their actions; most hadn't even insulated the loft. And despite the increasingly shrill warnings, large swathes of the population still apparently see no conflict in having children—whose lives could be blighted by global warming—and continuing to drive the 18 mpg [miles per gallon] Range Rover Sport and taking several long- and short-haul holidays per year. Climate change campaigners evidently need some help.

Peak Oil Will Soon Become a Personal Problem

Climate change arguments hold the moral high ground, but are weakened by the fact that their appeal is essentially altruistic: We are urged to change our ways for the sake of the polar bears now, and for other people mostly sometime in the future and a long way away. Peak oil by contrast appeals more immediately to baser instincts such as fear and self-preservation: What will happen to me and mine when the oil runs short? I concede these distinctions are being eroded as the news on global warming gets ever worse, but since those who flout climate change imperatives to cut their consumption are apparently selfish, perhaps peak oil is the best way to reach them. The climate change campaigner has nothing to match the wallet-grabbing power of the peak oil argument against buying an SUV [sport-utility vehicle]: How much do you think that beast will be worth with oil at $200 a barrel?

But if climate change campaigners were to take peak oil seriously, they would be forced to re-examine some of their most strongly held and comforting beliefs—and perhaps this is why some are so resistant. Once you accept a fairly imminent shortage of oil and liquid transport fuels—and thus a major hole in the entire energy supply—all sorts of unpleasant things follow. The idea that Western levels of consumption can continue to grow broadly as before becomes untenable. The idea of a system of progressively tighter energy rationing—along the lines of personal carbon trading—looks increasingly inevitable. The idea of natural gas as a 'bridge fuel' to some hydrogen-powered utopia looks ludicrous; gas production has already peaked in North America, is widely expected to peak in Europe by 2010, and some forecasters predict a global peak as early as 2025. And this in turn demands a cool reassessment of energy sources that many climate change campaigners have already rejected: coal-fired power stations with carbon capture and, I am sorry to say, nuclear power. Put this way, perhaps I have framed the question wrongly: Who wouldn't be afraid of oil depletion?

"Most arguments about peak oil are based on anecdotal information, vague references and ignorance of how the oil industry goes about finding fields and extracting petroleum."

Peaks in Global Oil Production Rates Will Not Be Reached for Many Years

Michael Lynch

Michael Lynch is the president and director of Global Petroleum Service at Strategic Energy & Economic Research, Inc., an energy market consulting firm. Lynch states in the following viewpoint that alarmists have invoked fears of peak oil for decades. According to Lynch, however, these fears are unfounded. Lynch claims that the world has many untapped oil reserves and that the oil industry is always improving ways of extracting more oil from existing deposits. He also insists that oil producers have continued to produce oil and weather market instabilities even during periods of global turmoil and warfare. In Lynch's view, oil is still abundant and will flow for many years to come.

As you read, consider the following questions:

1. As Lynch reports, in what year did Colin Campbell, the founder of the Association for the Study of Peak Oil & Gas, first assert the peak in oil production had been reached?

2. What are "superstraw" technologies, and how are they affecting oil fields, according to Lynch?

3. As Lynch states, how many trillion barrels of oil do geologists estimate are locked in the earth?

Remember "peak oil"? It's the theory that geological scarcity will at some point make it impossible for global petroleum production to avoid falling, heralding the end of the oil age and, potentially, economic catastrophe. Well, just when we thought that the collapse in oil prices since last summer [2008] had put an end to such talk, along comes Fatih Birol, the top economist at the International Energy Agency, to insist that we'll reach the peak moment in 10 years, a decade sooner than most previous predictions (although a few ardent pessimists believe the moment of no return has already come and gone).

Like many Malthusian beliefs [theories based on the notion that growing populations consume resources at an alarming rate], peak oil theory has been promoted by a motivated group of scientists and laymen who base their conclusions on poor analyses of data and misinterpretations of technical material. But because the news media and prominent figures like James Schlesinger, a former secretary of energy, and the oilman T. Boone Pickens have taken peak oil seriously, the public is understandably alarmed.

Fuzzy Logic Concerning Oil Reserves

A careful examination of the facts shows that most arguments about peak oil are based on anecdotal information, vague references and ignorance of how the oil industry goes about finding fields and extracting petroleum. And this has been demonstrated over and over again: The founder of the Association for the Study of Peak Oil [& Gas] first claimed in 1989 that the peak had already been reached, and Mr. Schlesinger argued a decade earlier that production was unlikely to ever go much higher.

Mr. Birol isn't the only one still worrying. One leading proponent of peak oil, the writer Paul Roberts, recently expressed shock to discover that the liquid coming out of the Ghawar field in Saudi Arabia, the world's largest known deposit, is around 35 percent water and rising. But this is hardly a concern—the buildup is caused by the Saudis pumping seawater into the field to keep pressure up and make extraction easier. The global average for water in oil field yields is estimated to be as high as 75 percent.

Another critic, a prominent consultant and investor named Matthew Simmons, has raised concerns over oil engineers using "fuzzy logic" to estimate reservoir holdings. But fuzzy logic is a programming method that has been used since I was in graduate school in situations where the factors are hazy and variable—everything from physical science to international relations—and its track record in oil geology has been quite good.

New, Untapped Reserves Exist

But those are just the latest arguments—for the most part the peak oil crowd rests its case on three major claims: that the world is discovering only one barrel for every three or four produced; that political instability in oil-producing countries puts us at an unprecedented risk of having the spigots turned off; and that we have already used half of the 2 trillion barrels of oil that the earth contained.

Let's take the rate-of-discovery argument first: It is a statement that reflects ignorance of industry terminology. When a

New Technologies Improve Oil Returns

One of the results of the more efficient means of research and development has been a far higher success rate in finding new oil fields. The success rate has risen in twenty years from less than 70 percent to over 80 percent. Computers have helped to reduce the number of dry holes. Horizontal drilling has boosted extraction. Another important development has been deep-water offshore drilling, which the new technologies now permit. Good examples are the North Sea, the Gulf of Mexico, and more recently, the promising offshore oil fields of West Africa. . . .

Thanks to new technologies, additional oil can now be recovered from the apparently exhausted reserves. Specifically, the peaking and declining of oil from an existing well is not the same as the peaking and declining of oil from the respective oil field or reservoir. While oil production from an existing well is bound to peak and then slow down, "offset wells" can be drilled later into the same field or reservoir to produce more oil.

Ismael Hossein-Zadeh, "The Recurring Myth of Peak Oil," Payvand's Iran News, October 1, 2008. www.payvand.com.

new field is found, it is given a size estimate that indicates how much is thought to be recoverable at that point in time. But as years pass, the estimate is almost always revised upward, either because more pockets of oil are found in the field or because new technology makes it possible to extract oil that was previously unreachable. Yet because petroleum geologists don't report that additional recoverable oil as "newly discovered," the peak oil advocates tend to ignore it. In truth, the combination of new discoveries and revisions to size estimates of older fields has been keeping pace with production for many years.

A related argument—that the "easy oil" is gone and that extraction can only become more difficult and cost-ineffective—should be recognized as vague and irrelevant. Drillers in Persia a century ago certainly didn't consider their work easy, and the mechanized, computerized industry of today is a far sight from 19th-century mule-drawn rigs. Hundreds of fields that produce "easy oil" today were once thought technologically unreachable.

The latest acorn in the discovery debate is a recent increase in the overall estimated rate at which production is declining in large oil fields. This is assumed to be the result of the "superstraw" technologies that have become dominant over the past decade, which can drain fields faster than ever. True, because quicker extraction causes the fluid pressure in the field to drop rapidly, the wells become less and less productive over time. But this declining return on individual wells doesn't necessarily mean that whole fields are being cleaned out. As the Saudis have proved in recent years at Ghawar, additional investment—to find new deposits and drill new wells—can keep a field's overall production from falling.

Political Instability Has Not Impacted the Oil Industry

When their shaky claims on geology are exposed, the peak oil advocates tend to argue that today's geopolitical instability needs to be taken into consideration. But political risk is hardly new: A leading Communist labor organizer in the Baku oil industry in the early 1900s would later be known to the world as Joseph Stalin.

When the large supply disruptions of 1973 and 1979 led to skyrocketing prices, nearly all oil experts said the underlying cause was resource scarcity and that prices would go ever higher in the future. The oil companies diversified their investments—Mobil even started buying up department stores!—and President Jimmy Carter pushed for the development of synthetic fuels like shale oil, arguing that markets were too myopic to realize the imminent need for substitutes. All sorts of policy wonks, energy consultants and Nobel Prize-winning economists jumped on the bandwagon to explain that prices would only go up—even though they had never done so historically. Prices instead proceeded to slide for two decades, rather as the tide ignored King Canute [who, in legend, tried to command the tide to stop rising along the shoreline].

Just as, in the 1970s, it was the Arab oil embargo and the Iranian Revolution, today it is the invasion of Iraq and instability in Venezuela and Nigeria. But the solution, as ever, is for the industry to shift investment into new regions, and that's what it is doing. Yet peak oil advocates take advantage of the inevitable delay in bringing this new production online to claim that global production is on an irreversible decline.

Oil Remains Abundant

In the end, perhaps the most misleading claim of the peak oil advocates is that the earth was endowed with only 2 trillion barrels of "recoverable" oil. Actually, the consensus among geologists is that there are some 10 trillion barrels out there. A century ago, only 10 percent of it was considered recoverable, but improvements in technology should allow us to recover some 35 percent—another 2.5 trillion barrels—in an economically viable way. And this doesn't even include such potential sources as tar sands, which in time we may be able to efficiently tap.

Oil remains abundant, and the price will likely come down closer to the historical level of $30 a barrel as new supplies come forward in the deep waters off West Africa and Latin America, in East Africa, and perhaps in the Bakken oil shale fields of Montana and North Dakota. But that may not keep the Chicken Littles from convincing policy makers in Washington [D.C.] and elsewhere that oil, being finite, must increase in price. (That's the logic that led the Carter administration to create the Synthetic Fuels Corporation, a $3 billion boondoggle that never produced a gallon of useable fuel.)

This is not to say that we shouldn't keep looking for other cost-effective, low-pollution energy sources—why not broaden our options? But we can't let the false threat of disappearing oil lead the government to throw money away on harebrained renewable energy schemes or impose unnecessary and expensive conservation measures on a public already struggling through tough economic times.

> "We can achieve strategic American energy independence and create more jobs and prosperity if we intelligently use our coal, oil and natural gas resources."

Energy Independence Is a Reachable Goal

George Allen

In the following viewpoint, George Allen argues that America can wean itself from foreign oil if the country wisely uses its own natural gas, oil, and coal resources. In his opinion, the U.S. government must oppose regulations that would limit carbon dioxide emissions, for these restrict the nation's use of its own fossil fuels. To ensure that these resources are not wasted, Allen stipulates that the country must embrace conservation of fossil fuels by improving vehicle fuel efficiencies and investing in clean coal technologies, nuclear power, and offshore natural gas drilling. Allen is a former U.S. senator and former governor of Virginia.

As you read, consider the following questions:

1. How much of America's energy needs are supplied by foreign imports, according to Allen?

George Allen, "Securing Our Economic Freedom," *Washington Times*, May 31, 2009.

2. Why does Allen believe that developing corn ethanol fuel is not an imperative for the nation?

3. What are "drop-in" fuels, as Allen explains, and what are their benefits to his energy scheme?

For decades, our presidents, Congress and unelected bureaucrats have passed legislation and regulations that have restricted access to our own resources, resulting in increased reliance upon foreign fuels to meet the energy needs of U.S. consumers and enterprise. We can achieve strategic American energy independence and create more jobs and prosperity if we intelligently use our coal, oil and natural gas resources, which are 85 percent of the energy that fuels our economy.

We need policies that encourage private investment, foster job creation, spur innovation and provide American consumers access to the vast, proven, affordable energy supplies under our land and water. These enormous taxpayer-owned resources, and the American jobs they would create, have been held hostage by almost 40 years of government policies saying, "No, we can't."

Informed Americans believe "Yes, we can!" We can achieve American energy freedom.

American energy policy finds itself at a crossroads. Either we will choose a future of abundant, affordable and reliable sources of American energy, or we can continue down the road of expensive, imported and highly regulated energy.

For a brighter energy future, we must stop five bad ideas and, initially, promote five positive, achievable goals for America.

- Specifically, for our American energy freedom, we must first play tenacious defense against harmful, costly and counterproductive burdens on America.

- Americans must oppose carbon and energy taxes, including "cap-and-trade" schemes established in some

"Oil on Mars.", cartoon by Ed Fischer. www.CartoonStock.com.

states and under debate in Congress. A federal cap-and-trade energy program would impose an additional $260 monthly burden on families with higher costs for electricity, clothes, food and fuel. German chancellor Angela Merkel recently said she would not allow European Union climate regulations that "would endanger jobs or investments in Germany." Our government must follow suit and vow to defend American jobs against the transfer of wealth from America for costly UN climate regulations.

- Halt the Environmental Protection Agency's [EPA's] attempt to regulate carbon dioxide using the Clean Air Act. That law was designed to regulate regional air pollutants, not global concentrations of carbon dioxide. Regulating carbon dioxide under this law is simply an attack on our large and abundant coal, natural gas and oil reserves. Consumers should demand that the federal government apply a cost-benefit analysis to any EPA proposal that attempts to address global temperatures.

- Oppose the attacks on America's largest energy source: coal. America gets 48 percent of its electricity from coal. Unlike wind and solar power, American coal is reliable, affordable and proven. Intermittent wind and solar cannot power our high-tech society's "always-on, ready-to-go" demand for base load electricity needs.

- Oppose unrealistic biofuel mandates that drive up the cost of our food and feed. Cellulosic ethanol may be a fuel of the future, but corn ethanol is jacking up the cost of food on our kitchen tables.

We must positively pursue the following five constructive reforms in federal energy policy:

- Embrace common-sense conservation and operational practices, teleworking, and more efficient equipment and building designs to save money and waste less energy. There are many practical innovations that reduce the energy needed to propel vehicles and heat, cool and illuminate government buildings as well as to better use water for landscaping.

- We should support clean coal technology for generating affordable electricity while providing jobs for Americans. By every measure—cost, availability, job creation and reliability—coal is by far the best energy source for base load electricity to fuel our economy.

- Enhance and develop the proven technology of coal-to-liquid fuels or coal synfuels. The Air Force successfully flight-tested coal-based jet fuel in bombers and fighter jets. Coal synfuel is a "drop-in" fuel that does not require engine modifications. South Africa and China have been moving forward with this clean, proven technology for coal synfuels; so should America. Under Governor Mitch Daniels's leadership, Indiana is pursuing new coal-to-gas technology to diversify the state's energy portfolio for electricity.

- Empower coastal states to take initiatives to safely explore the energy resources off their shores. Provide those willing states with 50 percent of revenue from offshore and onshore energy leasing. America is a much preferable source for natural gas than an unpredictable dependency on the foreign liquefied natural gas cartel.

- And we should remove outdated regulatory barriers to building the next generation of nuclear power plants. The federal government should allow nuclear fuel reprocessing, recycling, Pebble Bed Modular Reactors and other safe production of nuclear power.

If America adopted these positive reforms and innovations, we would unleash our creativity for American jobs, competitiveness, national security and American energy freedom!

> *"Unless or until America accepts the reality of the energy market, and America's interdependence with the Arab and OPEC worlds, then the idiotic political rhetoric—both Republican and Democratic—will continue."*

Energy Independence Is a Myth

Robert Bryce

Robert Bryce is the managing editor of Energy Tribune, *a monthly magazine devoted to the energy sector. Bryce is also the author of* Cronies: Oil, the Bushes, and the Rise of Texas, America's Superstate. *In the viewpoint that follows, Bryce states that those pundits and politicians who believe America can achieve energy independence are mistaken. Bryce points out that since 1949, the United States has relied more and more on imported oil and natural gas to furnish its fuel needs. In Bryce's opinion, Americans must realize that their nation—like every other country—is part of an interdependent, global energy network. Therefore, the government must shape wise policies that heed this reality instead of making vague, impractical promises about energy independence.*

Robert Bryce, "Idiotic Political Rhetoric About Oil: The Ongoing Myth of Energy Independence," *CounterPunch,*, November 21, 2006. Copyright © 2008 Counterpunch, LLP. Reproduced by permission.

As you read, consider the following questions:

1. Why does Bryce believe the neoconservatives in the government are calling for America to reduce its reliance on Arab oil?

2. In early 2006, how many barrels of foreign oil was the United States importing every day, as Bryce reports?

3. According to the author, why has America been reluctant to develop its own offshore oil reserves?

Now that the Democrats have swept aside the Republicans in both the House and the Senate, they are clamoring for major changes in policy. The first item on their list, rightly, is a change in America's military occupation in Iraq. They also want to raise the minimum wage and make prescription drugs more affordable. Bully for them. But the other item on their to-do list—energy independence—shows the profound, willful ignorance of American voters and their politicians.

The Call for Energy Independence

On November, 8 [2006], the new Speaker of the House, Nancy Pelosi, was on national television declaring that her party was going to be pushing for "energy independence and all that means."

To be fair, Pelosi isn't the only politico in the U.S. promoting the mirage of energy independence. A bunch of neoconservatives, led by pro-Iraq war militarists like Washington [D.C.] insider and super-hawk Frank Gaffney, former CIA [Central Intelligence Agency] director [R.] James Woolsey, and *New York Times* columnist Thomas [L.] Friedman, have also been pushing for more domestic production of ethanol and less reliance on imported oil—particularly the crude that comes from the Persian Gulf. For the neocons, and their allies in a new group called the Set America Free Coalition, buying less oil from the Persian Gulf will magically result in less terrorism in the U.S.

Of course, these calls for less foreign oil aren't new. Way back in 1970, a U.S. representative from Houston named George Herbert Walker Bush was declaring that America should be wary of oil imports. "This is particularly true now when instability in the Middle East severely threatens sources of our petroleum imports from that region of the world," he said. At the time when George Bush the Elder uttered those words, the U.S. was importing just 1.2 million barrels of crude oil per day and domestic producers were providing the majority of America's oil needs. In early 2006, the U.S. was importing nearly 10 million barrels of oil per day (about 60 percent of its needs) and George [W.] Bush the Younger was declaring that the U.S. was "addicted to oil" and thus, it should quit importing so much oil from the Persian Gulf.

America Needs Energy Imports

Alas, both of the George Bushes and their fellow politicos are ignoring the reality of the global market and the growing interdependence of the energy sector. For instance, in 2000, the U.S. imported less than 8 percent of its gasoline needs. By 2006, it was importing about 13 percent. America's imports of other motor fuels, including jet fuel and diesel, have also increased.

The U.S. needs more foreign natural gas, too. Canada, America's biggest gas supplier, has passed its peak gas production. Over the past two decades, as American gas fields have declined, U.S. imports of Canadian gas quadrupled. But Canada's gas production peaked in about 2002, and the country's gas output could fall by half over the next two decades. The decline in Canadian gas, coupled with America's ongoing hunger for natural gas, means that by 2010, the U.S. will be importing about 10 percent of its daily gas needs in

The Alternative Energy Economy Paradox

Despite its immense appeal, energy independence is a nonstarter—a populist charade masquerading as energy strategy that's no more likely to succeed (and could be even more damaging) than it was when [President Richard] Nixon declared war on foreign oil in the 1970s. Not only have we no realistic substitute for the oceans of oil we import, but many of the crash programs being touted as a way to quickly develop oil replacements—"clean coal," for example, or biofuels—come at a substantial environmental and political cost. And even if we had good alternatives ready to deploy—a fleet of superefficient cars, say, or refineries churning out gobs of cheap hydrogen for fuel cells—we'd need decades, and great volumes of energy, including oil, to replace all the cars, pipelines, refineries, and other bits of the old oil infrastructure—and thus decades in which we'd depend on oil from our friends in Riyadh [Saudi Arabia], Moscow, and Caracas [Venezuela]. Paradoxically, to build the energy economy that we want, we're going to lean heavily on the energy economy that we have.

Paul Roberts,
"The Seven Myths of Energy Independence,"
Mother Jones, May 1, 2008.

the form of LNG [liquefied natural gas]. Much of that gas will come from OPEC [Organization of the Petroleum Exporting Countries] countries like Qatar and Nigeria. By 2025, the Federal Energy Regulatory Commission expects LNG to account for 20 percent of America's daily gas consumption.

Making the matter even more absurd is that politicos of both parties, Republican and Democrat, have been restricting the expansion of oil exploration in America's coastal waters. The eastern Gulf of Mexico alone holds an estimated 20 trillion cubic feet of gas and 3.6 billion barrels of oil. But politicians from coastal states like Florida and Alabama don't want tourists to see drilling rigs when they go to the beach. So those resources are kept off-limits, even though they would help reduce America's need for imported energy. Further, those offshore resources are close to Texas and Louisiana where deepwater drilling is booming. And the technology and pipelines that are helping produce that offshore boom could easily be transferred to the eastern Gulf of Mexico.

The United States Is Part of a Global Energy Market

Despite all of these facts, American politicians continue to push the fantasy of energy independence, a world where ethanol made from corn (and, they hope, from switchgrass) will replace oil and American soldiers will never again need visit the Persian Gulf, except, perhaps, on vacation.

The truth is this: The last time the U.S. was independent of energy imports was 1949. Unless or until America accepts the reality of the energy market, and America's interdependence with the Arab and OPEC worlds, then the idiotic political rhetoric—both Republican and Democratic—will continue.

If Pelosi and the Democrats are serious about conserving oil and reducing imports, the most effective way is simple: Raise the federal fuel tax by a dime per gallon every year for the next ten years. It won't be politically popular but it's the best solution. Of course, observers shouldn't hold their breath while waiting for that tax to be implemented. Instead, they should brace themselves for (at least) two more years of inane discussions about energy by Washington insiders who know little—or nothing—about the reality of the modern energy business.

Periodical Bibliography

The following articles have been selected to supplement the diverse views presented in this chapter.

Ronald Brownstein   "On Energy, Let a Thousand Filaments Bloom," *National Journal*, March 28, 2009.

Laurel Graefe   "The Peak Oil Debate," *Economic Review*, vol. 94, no. 2, 2009.

Roger Howard   "Peak Oil and Strategic Resource Wars," *Futurist*, September 1, 2009.

Arthur B. Laffer   "Obama Should Forget About Energy Independence," *Wall Street Journal*, December 18, 2008.

Nicholas Newman   "Counting the Costs of Going Green," *Engineering & Technology*, July 21, 2009.

Mike Roberts   "Hydrogen Economy: Lead Balloon or a Load of Hot Air?" *TCE: The Chemical Engineer*, September 2009.

David Strahan   "Whatever Happened to the Hydrogen Economy?" *New Scientist*, November 29, 2008.

Bryan Walsh et al.   "Green Is the New Red, White and Blue," *Time*, April 28, 2008.

Kenneth T. Walsh   "Changing America's Energy Ways," *U.S. News & World Report*, April 1, 2009.

Michael E. Webber   "Three Cheers for Peak Oil!" *Earth*, June 2009.

OPPOSING
VIEWPOINTS®
SERIES

CHAPTER 2

What Alternative Energy Sources Should Be Pursued?

Chapter Preface

In early 2009, Mark Z. Jacobson, a professor of civil and environmental engineering at Stanford University, ranked alternative energy sources by their energy output, their sustainability, and their impact on human health and the environment. According to Jacobson, "The energy alternatives that are good are not the ones that people have been talking about the most. And some options that have been proposed are just downright awful." For example, he claims that the alternative fuel ethanol is environmentally unfriendly and simply may increase greenhouse gas emissions because of the need to plant, harvest, transport, and refine the fuel. Nuclear energy, on the other hand, does not produce much carbon dioxide, but spent nuclear fuel rods create problems in the form of storing hazardous waste.

In Jacobson's opinion, wind and concentrated solar power are the most promising alternative energies. Wind turbines require a relatively small plot of land and offset the carbon dioxide emitted during their manufacture by producing no carbon dioxide during their operating life. Similarly, concentrated solar energy would pay back its carbon investment in five to six months of operation. In addition, Jacobson believes these energy sources, put to use on a grand scale, could furnish enough power to meet specific demands. For example, wind power remains the best investment in Jacobson's view, because only 73,000 to 144,000 five-megawatt wind turbines would be required to charge up the entire fleet of vehicles in the United States if these automotives ran on electric battery power.

Jacobson also claims that wind turbines and solar energy collectors take less effort to plan and erect than do coal plants or nuclear reactors. Instead of waiting for years for the issuing of permits and the construction of large facilities, society would greatly benefit by building small-footprint wind farms and solar arrays that could begin generating energy and reducing carbon emissions quickly, Jacobson contends. Furthermore, he maintains that wind turbines and solar arrays are off-line for maintenance between 0 and 5 percent of each year, while the average coal plant is off-line for roughly 12 percent. That 12 percent is significant because a coal plant's downtime usually affects a large customer base; a wind or solar generator's downtime, however, would impact only a few users because they typically work in collective groups that do not all go off-line at the same time.

The supposed advantages of wind and solar power, however, are not universally recognized. In the following chapter, various experts assess the strengths and weaknesses of these and other alternative energy sources. They debate not only the potential impact of each on the environment—especially in terms of greenhouse gas production—but also the capability of each energy source to satisfy the increasing power requirements of the nation and the world.

> *"Just as we are blessed with good geology for coal, nature has also bestowed good geology for carbon storage."*

Clean Coal Can Supply U.S. Energy Needs

Gregory H. Boyce

Gregory H. Boyce argues in the following viewpoint that clean coal technology offers the greatest potential for U.S. energy independence and the reduction of carbon dioxide in the atmosphere. Boyce outlines the ways in which coal is a superior resource when compared with renewable energies such as solar and wind power. He explains the ways in which clean coal technology and carbon capture and storage—two methods of reducing the carbon emissions released during coal-based energy production— have revolutionized the coal industry and will eventually result in near zero-emission energy production. Boyce is the chairman and chief executive officer of Peabody Energy, the largest private-sector coal company in the world.

Gregory H. Boyce, "Why Black Is the New Green: The Enormous Potential of Clean Coal," *World Energy Magazine*, vol. 12, no. 1, 2009. Copyright © 2009 Loomis Publishing Services, Inc. Reproduced by permission.

read, consider the following questions:

Boyce reports, how much cheaper was the cost of
al than the cost of oil and natural gas in the United
States in 2008?

2. What are the two phases of clean coal in the United
States, as defined by Boyce?

3. According to Boyce, a century of carbon dioxide sequestration in the United States would use up what percentage of the geology potentially ripe for storage?

The character for "crisis" in Mandarin [Chinese] has two
meanings: danger and opportunity. As the world wrestles
with daunting energy, economic and environmental challenges,
this ancient wisdom offers a lesson for us all.

Our present economic crisis reminds us that affordable
energy is the foundation of our fragile global economy and
the engine of our recovery. Coal is our opportunity—the only
sustainable fuel able to meet enormous long-term energy
needs.

I have often heard coal called a "bridge to the future." To
this, I say: Coal is the future. Coal alone has the scale and cost
advantages to deliver what I call the "Three Es"—energy security, economic stimulus and environmental solutions. . . .

Coal Will Help to Power the World

While near-term energy demands are temporarily softened by
global economic conditions, the long-term outlook remains
strong, part of a sweeping transformation among developing
nations. World energy demand will grow 45 percent in the
next quarter century as massive infrastructure projects advance and billions of people gain access to electricity for the
first time, according to the International Energy Agency (IEA).
Global coal use is projected to increase 61 percent by 2030.
Demand for coal will grow more than the combined increase

in natural gas, nuclear, hydro, solar and wind consumption through 2025. China, India and the United States will lead this growth, expected to account for 90 percent of the increase in world coal demand into the foreseeable future.

The world needs all forms of energy to meet long-term demand, but each alternative has inherent limitations. The world's most productive oil fields are depleting. What oil is left is harder to find, more difficult to drill and more expensive to produce.

Major oil and natural gas supplies also come from unstable nations that are increasingly willing to use resources for political gain. For example, more than 80 percent of the world's natural gas is held in Russia, Iran and Venezuela. These are the same nations making headlines for pursuing an OPEC [Organization of the Petroleum Exporting Countries]-like natural gas cartel to control supply and price. Expanding the ability of a handful of nations in unstable regions to determine the world's energy destiny must be contrary to global energy security.

Other high-profile forms of energy remain too small or too scarce to provide energy at the scale needed to meet growing global needs. Coal plants generate electricity when clouds will not break for solar panels and when calm days quiet wind turbines. By the end of this year [2009], the U.S. Department of Energy will have spent more on solar and wind research in the past 30 years than the total inflation-adjusted cost of the Apollo space program. Yet the renewables portion of the U.S. energy portfolio has barely budged.

Solar and wind [power] combined still constitute 1 to 2 percent of U.S. electricity, and all renewable energy forms account for about 7 percent, roughly the same proportion reported by the Congressional Research Service 30 years ago. Even with the rapid growth of renewables, more than 80 percent of global energy consumed in 2030 will still come from conventional fuels, and only 2 percent of world primary energy is forecast to come from renewables, according to the IEA.

Coal and Energy Security

Coal's cost advantage is significant in 2008, for instance, the delivered cost of coal in the United States was 83 percent lower than oil and 79 percent lower than natural gas.

It is also important that nations not confuse conservation with recession. The secular trend toward greater energy use will continue—while the current underinvestment in energy will make supply-demand fundamentals all the more imbalanced when strong global economic growth inevitably resumes.

Because it is the world's most capital-intensive business, the energy industry acts much like a rubber band: When the economy contracts, generation projects stall, but when growth returns, demand comes roaring back. Without an increase in supply, nations around the world will compete for scarce supplies, and costs will again soar.

Coal is particularly attractive for nations increasingly seeking energy security that is put at risk from growing trends toward nationalization and protectionism. More than 200 gigawatts of electricity representing 700 million tons of annual demand are under construction in nations around the world. This drives enormous economic growth, representing more than 4.5 million jobs and $1 trillion in direct economic impacts.

Coal's versatility only adds to its attraction. New technologies allow coal to be transformed through "Btu [British thermal unit] conversion" applications into transportation fuels and natural gas.

Coal is mined commercially in more than 50 countries. Reserves are large and geographically diverse, from a variety of nations both large and small, developed and emerging, on ev-

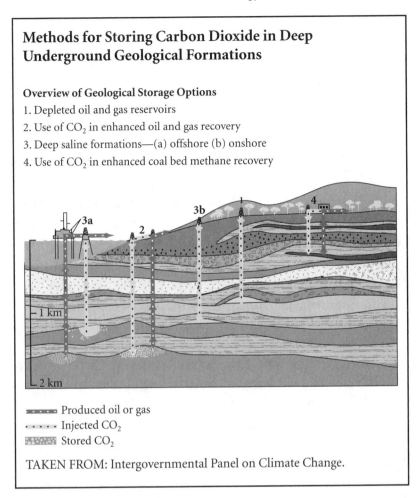

Methods for Storing Carbon Dioxide in Deep Underground Geological Formations

Overview of Geological Storage Options
1. Depleted oil and gas reservoirs
2. Use of CO_2 in enhanced oil and gas recovery
3. Deep saline formations—(a) offshore (b) onshore
4. Use of CO_2 in enhanced coal bed methane recovery

TAKEN FROM: Intergovernmental Panel on Climate Change.

ery major continent. Trade flows are well established. And in the words of the World Coal Institute, "Coal does not need high-pressure pipelines or dedicated supply routes that need to be protected at enormous expense." Coal can be easily stored, and coal-fueled electricity is well proven and not weather-dependent. . . .

The United States Moves Toward Clean Coal

Coal's vital role in energy security and economic stimulus carries over into environmental progress. Coal's improving environmental track record gives it a new green profile as the world's favorite fuel. Technologies that are now under development, too, are changing the color of coal, enabling us someday to achieve the ultimate green goal of near-zero emissions with carbon management.

That is why I like to say black is the new green. It is a statement that surprises some, inspires friends and intrigues the vast majority who hear it. But it also strikes at the core of the case for coal. So when the "why coal" question is answered and the follow-up turns to "how," the simple answer is: cleanly.

The United States demonstrates that clean coal comes in two distinct phases.

Phase one has already achieved impressive success. Utilities have invested tens of billions of dollars in clean coal technologies to eliminate emissions over the past several decades. As gross domestic product and electricity from coal have tripled in the United States since 1970, coal's environmental efficiency has dramatically improved, resulting in an 84 percent reduction of regulated emissions per ton of coal, based on an analysis of U.S. Environmental Protection Agency data.

Phase two—green coal—builds on this enormous progress, zeroing in on a reduced carbon footprint. New coal plants have a lower carbon-emissions rate than the existing fleet due to improved efficiency. This progress will continue in the United States and around the world with clean coal technology....

The Promise of Carbon Capture and Storage

Coal is ultimately a dense, high-energy product that makes it excellent for use in electricity generation and other end uses. This use results in the release of CO_2 [carbon dioxide]. Carbon capture and storage (CCS) technologies are under rapid development around the world, with the ultimate goal of near-zero emissions from coal-fueled generation. Technology is being advanced worldwide toward a low-carbon future that ultimately will capture and store carbon as part of a near-zero future.

The technologies separate the CO_2 from coal use and compress it into a fluid-like state that is as dense as liquid, making it easier and less costly to transport via pipelines. The CO_2 is injected deep underground in oil fields, caverns and saline fields, and deep beneath the ocean floor in geographic formations that have stored methane, coal and oil through the millennia. CCS is projected to be the lowest-cost low-carbon solution—less expensive than nuclear, wind or natural gas—according to a recent Carnegie Mellon University study.

The world has ample room for carbon storage. Just as we are blessed with good geology for coal, nature has also bestowed good geology for carbon storage. In the United States, for instance, we could sequester CO_2 for the next century and would not even use up 10 percent of the potential geology that is suitable for storage, based on an analysis by Pacific Northwest National Laboratory. There is enough capacity for hundreds of years of storage around the world.

CCS can also produce greater supplies of other energy. One of the most promising early applications for carbon storage is in aging oil fields for enhanced oil recovery. This process alone could lead to production of another 2 to 3 million barrels of oil per day in the United States, according to the National Coal Council.

Other promising technology paths beyond coal gasification include reducing CO_2 in an oxygen-rich environment during combustion or using scrubbing agents for removal.

The magnitude of the carbon challenge is enormous, and increased focus, funding and rules clarification all are needed. In a recent analysis of CCS, the IEA concluded that current spending levels are nowhere near enough to achieve deployment goals. I agree.

The development of CCS is not optional. In the words of former British prime minister Tony Blair: "The vast majority of new power stations in China and India will be coal-fired. Not may be coal-fired—will be. So, developing carbon capture and storage technology is not optional, it is literally of the essence."

We know that the world will use significantly more coal in the next several decades than it uses today. The question is whether that coal will be used in a low-carbon fashion. I say yes, with CCS. . . .

The Necessity of Developing Clean Coal

President Barack Obama may have summarized the need for coal best when he said: "Clean coal technology is something that can make America energy independent. This is America. We figured out how to put a man on the moon in 10 years. You can't tell me we can't figure out how to burn coal that we find right here in the United States of America and make it work."

The president recognizes that the era of vague and wishful policy prescriptions is over and that the moment for significant funding increases in all forms of energy—especially clean coal—is now. His message to Americans applies equally to the citizens of nations around the world. We must build the new coal plants and develop the coal-fueled technologies that create both jobs and low-cost energy, which in turn drives economies and improves lives. And we can do so while achieving our long-term carbon goals. The urgency of this message has never been so apparent.

It is time we recognize that the strength of our international economy is linked to our energy choices. We have the power to make change. Let's capitalize on the single resource that is most needed to deliver secure, affordable energy supplies and environmental solutions: our own willpower.

> *"Clean air standards have accelerated environmental destruction in West Virginia where low-sulfur coal is found beneath the earth's surface."*

Clean Coal Doesn't Exist

Kari Lydersen

In the following viewpoint, Kari Lydersen chronicles the environmental destruction resulting from the mining of coal in West Virginia. Lydersen argues that while clean coal technology may reduce carbon dioxide emissions, the mining of coal itself wreaks havoc on the environment from which the coal is extracted. The damage, notes the author, comes in the form of mountaintop removal, where entire mountaintops are dynamited or bulldozed into surrounding valleys in the search for coal, and the contamination of water sources from the runoff of coal-powered electric plants. Lydersen contends that the harmful effects of coal mining mitigate the benefits that clean coal technology could potentially provide. Lydersen is a journalist, author, and photographer whose work focuses on issues such as the environment, immigration, and free trade.

Kari Lydersen, "Dirtier Side Betrays Promise of 'Clean Coal,'" *New Standard*, March 15, 2006. © 2009 The New Standard. All rights reserved. Reproduced by permission of the author.

u read, consider the following questions:

1. As Lydersen recounts, in what ways was the town of Cheshire, Ohio, negatively impacted by the coal industry?

2. According to the author, how do plans for new coal-powered plants in Ohio address the reduction of carbon dioxide emissions by current plants?

3. What types of environmental damage does Lydersen claim clean air standards have caused in West Virginia?

On the West Virginia-Ohio border, the tread of the county's coal-burning power industry is expanding, digging into the Appalachian Mountains and kicking up clouds of pollution. While small towns choked by power plants hear the promise of new "clean coal" technologies, mining communities know there is no technological remedy for the destruction the industry is wreaking in their communities.

Though most people probably associate coal with the by-gone Industrial Age, the [George W.] Bush administration considers it an essential part of the nation's energy mix. At least 114 new coal-burning power plants are currently [as of 2006] in the building or permitting stages around the country. According to a 2006 report from the US Energy Information Administration, US power consumption from coal is expected to rise 1.9 percent per year through 2030, significantly more than the expected rise in energy consumption from petroleum (1.1 percent) and natural gas (0.7 percent).

Elisa Young, an aspiring organic farmer in Racine, Ohio, finds herself surrounded by this growing industry. Up to four new coal-burning plants are proposed for her area, even though her bucolic land is already ringed by smokestacks. Three major coal-burning power plants are visible from her farm, which has been in the Young family for seven generations. Within a short span of 20 miles, American Electric

Power (AEP) operates three power plants, and Ohio Valley Electric Corporation owns another.

Young would like to stay to farm her land, but she is up against an industry that would rather buy out the area than acquiesce to the health and environmental concerns of residents.

Coal Industry Plans for Expansion

About 15 miles away from the Young farm is the nearly abandoned Cheshire, Ohio, a stark reminder of the economic power of the coal-burning industry. In 2001, the Agency for Toxic Substances and Disease Registry (ATSDR) reviewed environmental data provided by the US Environmental Protection Agency around AEP's General John M. Gavin plant and concluded that "sulfur dioxide and sulfuric acid levels in and around Cheshire pose a public health hazard to some residents, particularly residents with asthma."

Under threat of a lawsuit, AEP bought nearly all the private property in the village for about $20 million in 2002—a price that gave most residents a deal well above property values.

Despite this record, AEP is proposing a new coal-burning plant in Meigs County and another across the river in New Haven, West Virginia, where it already runs the Mountaineer and Philip Sporn plants. American Municipal Power has also proposed a new plant in Meigs County, and a consortium of coal and energy companies called FutureGen, which includes AEP and coal giants Massey [Energy] and Peabody [Energy], is considering the area to locate an experimental new facility.

The Questionable Record of Clean Coal

The plants proposed by AEP would use a new technology known as integrated gasification combined cycle (IGCC) that boasts drastically reduced sulfur dioxide (SO_2), nitrogen oxide (NO_x) and mercury emissions. The companies advertise the

FutureGen plant as a zero emissions project, which would eliminate the SO_2, NO_x and mercury emissions and also sequester the greenhouse gas carbon dioxide (CO_2).

In addition to citing the need to build new plants to meet increased demand, AEP also says the state-of-the-art IGCC plants will create hundreds of jobs; for the Ohio plant alone, the company projects more than 1,000 temporary positions to open during construction followed by 125 permanent slots once the facility is running.

Local politicians and many residents welcome the plants.

"The economy's so bad, without the plants there's not much else," Karen Werry, a local historian and friend of Young, told *The New Standard* [TNS]. "I hate the pollution, but we need the jobs."

But Young isn't buying in.

While she is skeptical of the relatively untested clean coal technology and worried about the solid waste the plants will produce, Young's main concerns center on coal's dirty legacy. The plans for the new plants do not include any promises to reduce emissions at the existing plants. And nothing about zero-emissions technology can help her friends Larry Gibson and Maria Gunnoe across the river in West Virginia, where strip mining is permanently removing vast swaths of the mountain range to feed the nation's power plants.

Coal Mining Devastates the Environment

In fact, clean air standards have accelerated environmental destruction in West Virginia where low-sulfur coal is found beneath the earth's surface. With coal prices up and coal-fired power plants pegged by the Bush administration as the energy source of the future, strip mining in Appalachia is increasing at a fast pace.

Gibson's land in the once-lush Appalachian forest outside Charleston now looks more like New Mexico; an especially

The Coal Industry Spends Millions to Promote Clean Coal

The driving force behind coal's rebranding effort is the American Coalition for Clean Coal Electricity [ACCCE], a $40 million campaign funded by all the major components of the modern coal industry—mining companies, power plants, railroads, rural electric co-ops. ACCCE's ad blitz features sleek piano music and high-tech images of the globe; a panoply of workers voicing their belief in new technology; and, of course, President [Barack] Obama, speaking at a campaign stop in coal-rich southwestern Virginia. "This is America," Obama tells the crowd. "We figured out how to put a man on the moon in ten years. You can't tell me we can't figure out how to burn coal that we mine right here in the United States of America and make it work." The ad closes with Obama supporters chanting a familiar refrain: "Yes we can!" To promote its message, ACCCE hired a top ad firm out of [Las] Vegas and a well-connected Washington PR [public relations] outfit, spending three times as much last year [2008] as the health insurance industry did on the "Harry and Louise" ads in 1993–94 [ads run to oppose President Clinton's health care plan].

Ari Berman, "The Dirt on Clean Coal,"
Nation, April 13, 2009.

brutal form of strip mining known as "mountaintop removal" has turned it into a swath of bare mesas and plateaus dotted by oily sludge ponds.

His neighbor Gunnoe has seen the water in her well become totally undrinkable, contaminated with selenium, lime, arsenic and other toxins. The poison is delivered in runoff from two nearby containing ponds storing chemical waste produced by the cleaning of coal.

Young, Gibson and Gunnoe live at the intersection of environmental devastation from both ends of the coal-fired power industry: Mountaintop-removal miners have devastated more than 300,000 acres of West Virginia's rolling mountains by blasting it away or pushing it into adjacent valleys. Meanwhile, Ohio's array of coal-fired power plants is among the most concentrated in the country.

A 2005 report by the antipollution group Clear the Air found that the state ranked first in the country for sulfur dioxide and nitrogen oxide emissions in 2005 and second in the country for carbon dioxide (CO_2) emissions in 2003.

"We're definitely opposed to building more power plants in Ohio," said Erin Bowser, director of Ohio Public Interest Research Group. She told TNS that although the new proposals may be for facilities producing low or zero emissions, "they don't include anything about taking these older, dirtier coal plants off-line. We need to invest our resources in wind, solar and clean biomass energy instead. Ohio has tremendous wind potential that we're not taking advantage of."

Erasing a Region's History

Young herself is afraid that if nothing is done about the power plants, and if the new ones are built, the environment will become too unhealthy for her to stay at the farm no matter how much she loves it.

In the family cemetery on a hillside on the farm, she rubs the corroded surface of one gravestone. "This was here since the 1700s, and when I was a kid you could still read it," she said. "Not now, because of the contamination in the air. They're erasing our family history, literally. Kids call the plants 'cloud factories.' Clouds that can kill you."

Though mining and coal-fired power plants are inextricably linked, Young notes that many people don't acknowledge that connection. Even prominent clean-air and environmental groups, including the American Lung Association and the Natural Resources Defense Council, often speak out in favor of "clean coal" technology like IGCC. But critics insist clean coal is a red herring that might improve air quality but still creates a host of serious health and environmental problems.

"It's like a Pandora's box," Young says of her growing awareness of the coal industry's harmful effects. "Now when I see these piles of coal I just think of mountains and cry."

> "Not only is marginal land a useful op-
> portunity in many places for biomass
> production, the substitution of nonre-
> newable inputs (such as fertilizers) with
> renewable inputs (such as compost)
> further improves sustainability."

Plants Used in Manufacturing Biofuels Can Be Cultivated on Unused Lands

Paul Bardos et al.

The use of crops to produce fuel has become an increasingly popular method of alternative energy production in recent debate. In the viewpoint that follows, Paul Bardos and his colleagues argue that marginal lands—degraded, unused lands—provide the ideal location to plant crops to be used in the production of biofuels. These researchers contend that many acres of unused lands that have been damaged by past industrial endeavors are now sitting idle. The authors argue that such lands could finally be put back into use and that the cultivation of biofuel crops on these marginal lands will not only rejuvenate the soil in which the crops are grown, but also improve the economies of the surrounding communities. Bardos works for the British environmental and waste management research consulting company r3 Environmental Technology Ltd. His colleagues, who served as coauthors of this viewpoint, are researchers at other European environmental and biotech firms.

As you read, consider the following questions:

1. What are some of the industrial activities cited by the authors that have affected the previously developed lands in Europe?

2. What are some of the benefits the authors believe can be derived from biomass production on land where food cultivation is not appropriate?

3. According to the authors, what three factors must be considered when evaluating marginal land use?

The increasing importance of biomass for energy production and feedstock for manufacturing processes (e.g., plastics) has become a worldwide phenomenon. Establishment of non-food crops for biomass can contribute to policy goals related to renewable energy and carbon management. However, use of land to produce any type of biomass for feedstock, fuels and energy has become increasingly contentious, with a range of concerns about impacts on food production and habitat (conservation issues). There is also the question about whether some biofuels even have a positive carbon balance at all when the effects of biomass cultivation on nitrous oxide emissions from soil are considered. The wider environmental impacts on soil and water and the carbon and resource costs of artificial fertilizers and pesticides also are factors.

A European Environment Agency (EEA) Scientific Committee has questioned the sustainability of existing European Union (EU) commitments to biofuels, and suggested that the EU target to increase the share of biofuels used in transport to

10 percent by 2020 should therefore be suspended. This suggestion was echoed by the European Parliament in September 2008, although it is not yet clear if this argument has been accepted by the European Commission [EC]. The EEA opinion was in part based on a sustainable land use report it commissioned, which found that in 2005 an estimated 36,000 km² [square kilometers] of agricultural land in the 25 EU member countries were directly devoted to biomass production for energy use, projected to rise to 190,000 km² by 2030.

An Abundance of Degraded Land

Use of marginal land and secondary resources (such as compost, biosolids and other recycled organics as a soil input, and other resources such as agricultural and forestry residues as a source of biomass) is an emerging opportunity in this biomass debate. Marginal land includes previously developed land, underutilized land and land affected by diffuse contamination. All across Europe there are areas of land that have been degraded by past use, and that are not possible to restore easily or sustainably using conventional methods. Such previously developed land includes areas affected by mining, fallout from industrial processes such as smelting [extracting metal from ore through a melting process], activities related to forestry and the pulp and paper industry, areas elevated with contaminated dredged sediments, former landfill sites and many other areas where the decline of industrial activity has left a legacy of degraded land and communities. The extent of contamination may not be sufficient to trigger remediation under current regulatory conditions, and there may be little economic incentive to regenerate the areas affected.

In August 2007 the EEA estimated that some 250,000 sites in EU member countries require cleanup, and that potentially polluting activities may have taken place at 3 million sites. Numbers are set to rise. A relatively high proportion of these sites remain unused because of problems that include contamination, market failure, cost and planning difficulties. For example, United Kingdom (UK) data from 2005–07 suggests there is 63 km² of previously developed land in England, of which 35 km² were vacant or derelict; 17 km² had been derelict for more than 9 years (sites larger than 2 hectares). A UK regional study in the northwest of England identified 15 km² of previously developed land, however, this area increased to 26 km² if "underutilized/neglected" land was included.

Data about areas of land affected by diffuse contamination are harder to find. However, in areas like Avonmouth, UK, De Kempen, Belgium and the Netherlands, and the Nord-Pas-de-Calais, France, many square kilometers of land are affected by smelter fallout alone, and thousands of square kilometers are suspected to be contaminated in Eastern Europe, e.g., Lithuania and Ukraine.

Returning Productivity to Marginal Lands

Food cultivation may not be appropriate on marginal land, for example, because of public concerns over the possible presence of soil contaminants. However, not only is marginal land a useful opportunity in many places for biomass production, the substitution of nonrenewable inputs (such as fertilizers) with renewable inputs (such as compost) further improves sustainability—the combination of cultivation and soil rehabilitation could be an integral part of land rehabilitation and risk management in the long term. There may also be further benefits from this kind of land use, e.g., providing a self-funding land management regime, returning economic activity to deprived areas, a long-term improvement in land values and environmental benefits such as carbon sequestration (substitution of fossil carbon resources, and "temporary" sequestration in managed soils), depending on the area. The renewable energy opportunities presented by marginal land use have been recognized by the US EPA [Environmental Protection Agency].

Of course, set against the scale of agricultural land use overall, the marginal land bank may not seem large. However, using it as a biofeedstock resource is important for several reasons: The land bank may be very significant in particular localities and regions, and these are often areas with economic underperformance; it is an effective means of returning productivity to marginal land; and it brings wider sustainability benefits.

Evaluating and Restoring Marginal Land

Factors to consider when evaluating marginal land are: 1) Fit for purpose, e.g., manage the risks posed by the contamination; 2) Sustainable, i.e., with small environmental impacts and low use of resources and energy, providing economic benefit rather than stringent costs and wider social benefits; and 3) Attractive to implement, i.e., low cost needing little active management, are readily acceptable to land owners, authorities and the public, stimulating interest. It is possible that long-term use of marginal land for biomass production may at least offset the costs of its management, and potentially even generate local revenue.

The use of recycled organic matter for biomass production on marginal land is likely to fall into two stages. The first is the conditioning and restoration to create conditions suitable for biomass production. The second might be ongoing additions for maintaining soil productivity and fertilizer substitution. Depending on the biomass being grown, this reuse of organic matter such as compost is likely to be far greater in terms of volume required per unit area than the single applications of compost conventionally used for the restoration of marginal land, such as for public amenity use—"country parks" and nature areas—that has characterized a large amount of marginal land management in the past. This is potentially a significant outlet for recycled organic matter.

Crops to Restore Marginal Land

Some biofuel crops can grow on degraded land and help restore its productivity. One example is switchgrass, which may even improve soil quality and productivity. It can have eight times higher below-ground biomass and as much as 55% more total soil organic carbon than corn/soybean over two rotations. The use of leguminous nitrogen-fixing plants is an option to improve soil fertility. Jatropha may also improve soil quality and can grow under less optimal conditions, perhaps enabling the planting of other crops over time. However, it has yet to be empirically proven at which scale jatropha production may provide a net benefit.... Halophytic crops thrive in relatively high-saline areas, such as some deserts and in coastal areas, where major crop species are unable to grow. During their growth, salt is taken up. Such crops could clean soils of high salinity, although saline agriculture is still in its infancy and research on ecologically sound cultivation of marsh crops is ongoing. Finally, soil contaminated with heavy metals (comprising about 10,000 ha [hectares] in the USA and Europe) could be restored by growing energy crops that take up these pollutants.

Stefan Bringezu et al., "Assessing Biofuels:
Towards Sustainable Production and Use of Resources,"
United Nations Environment Programme, 2009.

Assessing the Viability of Marginal Lands for Biofuel Crops

Opportunities for combining marginal land reuse, organic matter recycling, risk management and biomass production are being explored by the European "Rejuvenate" project, which will: evaluate the feasibility of a range of possible approaches to combining risk-based land management (RBLM) with non-food crop land uses and organic matter reuse as appropriate; develop a decision support tool to identify marginal land for biomass reuse opportunities in the UK, Germany and Sweden; and assess how verification of their performance might be carried out and identify what requirements remain for future research, development and demonstration.

"Rejuvenate" includes partners from Germany, the UK, the Netherlands and Sweden and began in October 2008. It is funded, under the umbrella of an ERA-Net SNOWMAN [sustainable management of oil and groundwater under the pressure of soil pollution and soil contamination], by the Department for Environment, Food and Rural Affairs and the Environment Agency (England), Formas [Swedish Research Council for Environment, Agricultural Sciences and Spatial Planning] (Sweden) and Bioclear BV (Netherlands). The [European Commission's] EU ERA-Net SNOWMAN is a network of national funding organizations and administrations providing research funding for soil and groundwater, bridging the gap between knowledge demand and supply (www.snowman -era.net). It is one of more than 70 ERA-Nets (European Research Area-Networks) funded by the EC's 6th Framework Programme for Research and Technological Development.

The "Rejuvenate" project will identify generic opportunities for and barriers to combining non-food crop production with risk-based land management for economically marginal degraded land (i.e., areas of degraded land that have remained underutilized for protracted periods of time). Opportunities will be categorized based on compatibility with land risk management requirements; land characteristics; biomass applications and markets; and organic matter reuse opportunities.

Determining Profitability, Compatibility, and Amenity

Opportunities will be assessed for their likely levels of profitability and project risk, know-how requirements, compatibility with other forms of reuse (such as built development) and amenity. For bioenergy crops, particular attention will be paid to "second generation" biofuel opportunities. First generation biofuels such as ethanol from maize tend to process commodities, which can also be used as foods. Second generation biofuels are derived from residues such as straw or the entire crop biomass, e.g., including lignocellulosic components, and are seen as offering higher energy yield per unit land area with lower environmental impacts. Opportunities will also be assessed for their state of development, identifying what verification measures might be required to appraise human health risk management and wider sustainability factors such as carbon sequestration potential and local revenue generation potential.

A combination of considerations will allow an approximate ranking of the likely attractiveness of different RBLM and non-food crop approaches on the basis of long-term viability. Key factors are likely to be: maintenance of a productive soil (including whatever soil forming processes are needed at the beginning); local climatic and meteorological conditions; meeting crop requirements, particularly with a view to minimizing or substituting nonrenewable inputs and inputs that might have wider environmental impacts such as persistent pesticides; maximizing the "carbon value" of soil management and production, considering permanent sequestration by the substitution of nonrenewable inputs by the biomass produced, and temporary sequestration within the managed site surface; and providing an effective means of combining non-food reuse with concerns about biodiversity and ecological impacts and public amenity values (such as landscape and accessibility).

Regulations governing restoration of marginal lands using organic waste materials vary from country to country, but two considerations will be important: quality of the biomass produced and effective management of risks to human health and the wider environment.

Risk Management Plans

The transfer of potential contaminants from the marginal land (or secondary organic matter inputs) to biomass needs to be avoided, or at least be limited to levels tolerable by downstream biomass use (for energy, fuel or manufacturing feedstock). This consideration is important both from a competitive product quality standpoint, and to avoid triggering a regulatory view that the feedstock generated is a waste or its use of downstream processing needs special pollution control measures.

Risks to human health and the wider environment from the marginal land and secondary organic matter inputs must be managed with local regulatory requirements or better. These risks might include toxic substance transfer to biomass, risks to human health of toxic substances by direct contact with contaminated surfaces or via blowing dust. There are also other environmental risks such as nitrate migration to groundwater. Risk management needs will be highly site and material specific. It is also likely that pragmatic risk management strategies will be adopted—driven by finding the approach that is most likely to win regulatory acceptance and is most economically feasible, both of which are vital to securing rapid reuse of the marginal land.

"Genuinely marginal land, land that is not vital to local communities, does not exist in the amounts assumed."

Biofuel Cultivation Will Harm the Environment and Marginalize Populations

Helena Paul

In the following viewpoint, Helena Paul questions the existence of the marginal land—supposedly unused wasteland that exists worldwide—touted by agrofuel proponents as the ideal location to plant crops used for biofuels. Paul outlines the many ways in which these allegedly decimated lands are in fact essential to the communities that surround them, especially in developing countries. She claims that often marginalized, underrepresented populations such as women, pastoralists, and the impoverished depend on this land for survival and would not receive any of the benefits resulting from the conversion of the land for the cultivation of agrofuel crops. Additionally, Paul states that because the efficacy of biofuels as a replacement for traditional fuels has not been proven, the transformation of marginal lands to agrofuel plantations could yield limited or no reduction in fossil fuel use.

Helena Paul, "Biofuels 2.0," *Ecologist*, vol. 39, no. 1, February 2009, pp. 14–21. This article first appeared on www.theecologist.org in February, 2009. Copyright © 2009 MIT Press Journals. Reproduced by permission.

Paul is an advocate of indigenous people's rights. She is also co-director of EcoNexus, a public research institute and science watchdog based in Great Britain, and co-author of the book Hungry Corporations: Transnational Biotech Companies Colonise the Food Chain.

As you read, consider the following questions:

1. Paul claims that proponents of agrofuel define marginal land using what terms to make what suggestion?

2. According to Paul, how would the pastoralists of Africa be negatively impacted by the conversion of "marginal lands" to agrofuel plantations?

3. What does Paul identify as the negative environmental impact of converting marginal land in Africa from grazing area to agrofuel crop production?

Recent months have seen intense debate over agrofuels—biofuels made from crops. At first they were described as a panacea, a means of addressing climate change and regenerating agriculture and rural regions in Europe and around the world, particularly in Africa. The drive to exploit the global south for production of fuels from food crops such as corn and soya was presented as a development opportunity. However, many questions have since arisen about their true value for reducing greenhouse gas emissions and their impact on food production and prices. The indirect impacts of agrofuel production, such as land-use change, water depletion, waste, the displacement of people, other crops and animals and the human and environmental costs entailed, have become major concerns.

In response, policy makers have been offered "second generation" agrofuels. These, we are told, will not affect food production because they will use non-food crops. Technologies will convert the [whole] plant or tree to fuel, not just the fruit or seed. At least that is the vision. However, large plantations will still be required to provide the raw materials and thus, although agrofuels might not compete for food crops, they will certainly compete for land and water. Moreover the technologies may not be commercially viable for 10–20 years. . . .

Marginal Land Is Not Really Marginal

For a start, where is this marginal land that is now presented to us as a solution to current agrofuel problems and the need to expand agricultural production in general? How is it defined? This is a key question, because, as well as marginal, it is variously described as degraded, underused, abandoned, sleeping, wasteland. These pejorative terms are being widely used to suggest that millions of hectares would benefit from being converted to agrofuel plantations. For example, the Brazilian government asserts that sugarcane in Brazil is mainly planted on "degraded" land, of which it claims there are millions of hectares.

There is a resounding response to such assertions in *Mausam*, a new Indian magazine on climate change on the Corner House Web site, which says: "Rural and forest communities [. . .] say that there is no such thing as wastelands. Most of these lands are grazing lands, common pastures, degraded forests and also lands of small and marginal communities. They not only support a multitude of livelihoods but also have a critical ecological role. This is where the government and corporations are pushing for their fuels, displacing thousands of peoples [. . .]

"Pastures and grazing lances in India are often de facto village commons and CPRs (common property resources), many of which form part of the larger forest landscapes and contribute to the forest communities' economy and livelihoods." According to *Mausam* there are millions of hectares of such land in India, vital to local people.

Agrofuel Production Could Marginalise Women

As soon as one looks at marginal land in this way, it becomes clear that the pattern is repeated worldwide: Untitled, common land exists in Africa, South America and across Asia. People may farm a plot individually, but also depend upon the shared resources of the commons. Indeed such land was a vital resource in the UK [United Kingdom] until the great waves of enclosure that reached a climax in the 19th century dispossessed and uprooted ordinary people, concentrating land in the hands of a few, driving the majority into cities.

Genuinely marginal land, land that is not vital to local communities, does not exist in the amounts assumed. There are therefore highly damaging assumptions being made, about the true extent of marginal lands available.

Jonathan Davies, global coordinator of the World Initiative for Sustainable Pastoralism, Nairobi, Kenya, says: "In Africa, most of the lands in question are actively managed by pastoralists, hunter-gatherers and sometimes dryland farmers [...] There may be wastelands lying around to be put under the plough, but I doubt that they are very extensive." In many parts of the world, women still have no property or inheritance rights. So-called marginal land may be the only land they can access. Widows, for instance, are sometimes given degraded land on which to grow food.

For them, it can make the difference between life and death in hard years because they know how to produce and gather food from it. Thus, according to the UN's [United Nations] Food and Agriculture Organization 2008 report, *Gender and Equity Issues in Liquid Biofuels Production—Minimizing the Risks to Maximize the Opportunities*: "The conversion of these lands to plantations for agrofuels production might therefore cause the partial or total displacement of women's agricultural activities towards increasingly marginal lands," which would apply even greater pressure on women and land alike. Female labour on plantations is often exploitative and insecure while men usually benefit the most from cash crops for export.

Ignoring Land Use by Pastoralists

Another group regularly marginalised in discussions about development are cattle herders and pastoralists, especially in Africa. They travel across wide areas following the seasonal rains and fresh grass with their animals. External observers often assume that their lives would be improved if they were settled in one place and provided with the means to grow crops. However, the pastoralist way of life, evolved over many generations, often embodies vital knowledge about how to sustain these fragile resources.

At the 11th session (2005) of the Working Group on Minorities from the higher Commission on Human Rights, an Ethiopian representative said: "The pastoral groups of the region traditionally depend on the common property resources consisting of pasture, water and mineral licks. Each has management rules that regulate access and responsibilities. Customarily, land is the collective property of the pastoralists and managed according to specific rules." Pastoralist communities in particular use highly effective systems of traditional ecological governance to manage their environments, but these are rarely acknowledged in modern development thinking.

Such collective management of land is often invisible to outsiders—whether government or private capital. The convenient concept of *terra nullius*—empty land—continues to thrive. The briefing *Agrofuels and the Myth of the Marginal Lands*, published in September 2008 by the Gaia Foundation [an environmental organisation] and others, reports: "Icin, an indigenous Dayak from West Kalimantan, Indonesia points at a map of the proposed [agrofuel] plantations, on supposedly unproductive 'sleeping' land. 'Actually there should be seven

Tariffs Limit the Economic Benefits of Biofuel Production

The many sustainable development potentials associated with biofuels are contingent upon international trading, since the most efficient producing countries are or will be developing countries, while the main consumers are industrialised countries. The bad news is that, under current trading conditions, there are several policy problems preventing developing countries from reaping the benefits of the biofuels trade, not to mention the negative environmental and social impacts that these policies may have.

Several trade barriers distort biofuel trade and jeopardise developing countries' potential to benefit from greater global demand for biofuels. Tariff barriers commonly insulate domestic producers from external competition. The United States, for example, applies an extra US$0.54 to each gallon of imported bioethanol on top of the 2.5 percent tariff, bringing the cost of Brazilian bioethanol in line with that produced domestically. Moreover, the tariff escalation systems that prevail in many industrialised countries encourage developing countries to export feedstock, such as unprocessed molasses and crude oils while the final biofuel conversion—and associated value addition—takes place in the importing country. The tariffs vary—the EU [European Union] and United States, for instance have trade agreements granting preferential market access conditions for certain countries and products.

Annie Dufey, "International Trade in Biofuels: Good for Development? And Good for Environment?"
Environment for the MDGS, *January 2007.*

villages marked in this area. But they are not mentioned. Does this mean, for the outside world, we do not exist anymore?'"

Agrofuel Production May Not Benefit Native Farmers

Where convenient, the presence of people may be recognised by agrofuel proponents. Smallholder farmers are often cited as the likely beneficiaries of agrofuel developments, especially oil palm and jatropha, because these require labour, but according to Olivier De Schutter, United Nations Special Rapporteur on the right to food, in his report to the UN General Assembly: "There is a real risk that export-led agricultural development will further marginalise the position of smallholders, worsening their food in security instead of improving it."

Thus land that might appear "marginal" to one person can be a vital resource to another. It may seem idle, degraded or underused, yet can provide vital food, fuel, medicine and building materials to local communities; it may be collective or common land used by such communities for generations, without the security of formal title to it.

Yet, as De Schutter notes: "No governmental delegation present at the High-Level Conference on World Food Security [held in June 2008 as the food crisis increased] mentioned agrarian reform or the need to protect the security of land tenure." Land reform is constantly sidelined by governments, but becomes ever more urgent in the context of agrofuels. This is because, while there is a natural limit to the demand for food crops, demand for agrofuel crops is potentially inexhaustible, because of the enemy dependence of industrialised countries and the fact that fossil fuel is far more energy-dense than biomass. Even if agrofuel growers benefit, "food security might suffer, for instance as a result of the increased price of land or a diminished availability of food."

De Schutter warns against trying to shape development through export crops, yet this is exactly how the agrofuel agenda is promoted in many regions.

Converting Grazing Land to Cropland

The interaction between people and marginal land may be subtle and complex. Dr Melaku Worede, a renowned Ethiopian geneticist, one of the founders of Seeds of Survival [a program to expand the genetic diversity and hardiness of crops in Ethiopia] and a specialist in uncultivated biodiversity, says that marginal land with poor soils can be home to a highly biodiverse population of plants and animals in dynamic interaction. In parts of Ethiopia, these lands are not actively managed, and small farmers frequently leave areas undisturbed alongside the fields they cultivate. Although little studied, such marginal areas may prove to be important reserves. Because plants on marginal land must continuously adapt to harsh, often rapidly changing conditions, such land could be a vital source of genetic diversity for resistance to stresses such as drought, disease and pests in the future, especially as climate change threatens the viability even of locally adapted crops.

It is deeply ironic that climate change, already a serious threat to biodiversity and food production, may be accelerated by the conversion of marginal land to crops for biofuels— ostensibly to tackle climate change. Yet, while there is some discussion about how changes in land use increase global greenhouse gas emissions, for example when forests are cleared for crop production, we hear less about localised climate change caused by land-use change. Projections indicate that changing from grazing to crop production in East Africa would make some areas wetter and others drier, with more extreme floods and droughts and greater temperature differentials. The Web site of the International Livestock Research Institute reports that a joint African/US initiative, the Climate

Land Interaction Project, "provides evidence of the complex connection between regional changes in climate and changes in land cover and land use. New study results are warning that the conversion of huge areas of pasturelands to croplands in east Africa will be a major contributor to global warming in the region." And this for the continent already projected to suffer some of the worst impacts of global climate change.

Yet the pressure for a "green revolution" for Africa and the perception that it is the "new agricultural frontier" could lead to the rapid and violent conversion of pasture and other "marginal" lands to crops. It also provides a good pretext for land-grabbing, as prices are set to rise. The market is certainly taking an interest. Mark Twain once quipped: "Buy land: they're not making it any more." Recognising that agriculture may be entering a period of scarcity and hence high prices, and also fleeing the property downturn, speculators and corporations have moved into land and crop commodities. Indeed speculation and hoarding were at least partly to blame for high food prices in recent months. Hedge funds and corporations have also recognised the opportunity for profits. Emergent Asset Management, based in the UK, recently launched its African Agricultural Land Fund, inviting investors to participate in "the growing sub-Saharan agricultural sector." In its 2007 report, *Agrofuels in Africa: The Impacts on Land, Food and Forests*, the African Biodiversity Network found that cases of "land grabbing" had accelerated with the new influx of agrofuel developments.

Marginal Land Conversion Could Marginalise Human Survival

Even the US and the EU [European Union] are not immune to the "marginal land" issue. In some cases, land set aside in the EU and conservation reserve land in the US may be "marginal" because it is dry, has poor soils or steep gradients—yet may have a vital function within the ecosystem. For example, the US Conservation Reserve Program has been extremely successful in protecting biodiversity and water, reducing soil erosion and providing natural flood control. According to US government figures, it prevents 408 million tonnes of soil erosion and sequesters nearly 21 million tonnes of carbon a year. Yet across the US and EU, millions of hectares of previously set-aside land (approximately 10 percent of the cropland in each region) are now being planted, following pressure from the agroenergy lobby and high commodity prices, which agrofuels have helped to push up.

To focus on "marginal" land for agrofuels is extremely risky. Such land can be a vital resource for local people, who are often its most effective managers, yet they may be invisible to corporations and policy makers, conveniently so for corporate agendas. Marginal land often plays a key role in protecting biodiversity, water and soil. That there are interactions between land-use change and climate change is clear but the dynamics are little understood. One thing is certain: They go far beyond the facile and deceptive emission counting beloved of bureaucrats and carbon traders. We already face an unpredictable future with increased extremes of temperature, rainfall winds, droughts and violent weather events. Biodiverse ecosystems have a critical role to play in stabilising climate. And as far as plant genetic resources are concerned (a dry term for something our lives depend on!), so-called marginal land could be crucial. It must not be recklessly drenched in fertilisers and chemicals and planted with crops for unproven fuels in an attempt to avoid genuine adaptation to the end of the fossil fuel age and energy dense consumption patterns. If we do not act responsibly, we could further marginalise our survival. This is no idle threat.

| *"There are no physical or practical limits that would prevent renewable resources from one day providing all of the world's energy."*

Renewable Energy Sources Can Meet America's Energy Demands

Chris Flavin and Janet Sawin

Unlike fossil fuels that will eventually run out, renewable energy sources can be continually tapped for their energy-generating potential. These sources include the sun, wind, ocean, and geothermal power. In the viewpoint that follows, Chris Flavin and Janet Sawin explain the benefits of each of these sources and argue that renewables have the potential to generate sufficient energy to power the world. Flavin and Sawin contend that recent demand for renewable sources has led to price decreases and technical advances that will eventually make this technology cheaper and cleaner than fossil fuels. They hope that political support will help ensure the adoption of renewable energy sources as the proper energy alternative for America. Flavin is the president of Worldwatch Institute, an international research organization

Chris Flavin and Janet Sawin, "Renewables: What We Meant to Say," *World Watch*, vol. 20, January/February 2007, pp. 2–4. Copyright 2007, www.worldwatch.org. Reproduced by permission.

dedicated to advancing sustainable energy supplies and protecting the environment. Sawin is a senior researcher at Worldwatch Institute.

As you read, consider the following questions:

1. How many gigawatts of power does the U.S. Department of Energy estimate that offshore U.S. wind power is capable of generating, and what percentage of current U.S. generating capacity does this equal?

2. What two factors do the authors believe have limited the deployment of renewable energy to date?

3. According to the authors, by what percentage did the production of wind turbines and solar photovoltaics increase in 2005?

Our conclusion that renewable energy, combined with high levels of energy efficiency, is a robust alternative to fossil fuels is based on scientific and engineering studies that document the vast scale of the renewable energy resource base—including solar, wind, geothermal, and biological resources—as well as the rapid advance in energy conversion technologies now under way.

An Abundance of Wind and Solar Power

Wind power is a good example. A 1991 study by the Pacific Northwest National Laboratory found that land-based wind resources in just three states could theoretically meet all U.S. electricity needs, even with significant environmental, urban, and other exclusions. Since then, wind power technology has advanced significantly, and wind turbines can now be used to capture the stronger, more consistent winds offshore. The U.S. Department of Energy estimates the offshore U.S. wind potential (within 5–50 nautical miles) at 900 gigawatts (GW), equal to 92 percent of current U.S. generating capacity. Researchers at Stanford University recently concluded that previous studies have considerably underestimated wind's potential because they did not take into account the higher-altitude winds that can be reached with modern wind turbines. The Stanford researchers estimated global wind energy potential at 72,000 GW. This means that, with current technology, wind could supply more than 10 times as much electricity as the world now uses. No one expects the world to rely on a single source of electricity, but the evidence is clear that wind power can provide a larger share of electricity than either nuclear or hydropower do today.

Solar energy is even more abundant. The solar energy striking the surface of the earth each day is sufficient to meet the world's electricity needs for an entire year. Researchers at the National Renewable Energy Laboratory and Platts Research and Consulting estimate that just seven states in the U.S. southwest could provide more than 7,000 GW of solar generating capacity—nearly seven times the nation's existing electric capacity from all sources. A little more than 10,000 square kilometers—equivalent to 3.4 percent of the land in New Mexico—could produce 30 percent of current U.S. electricity, enough to replace half the coal now used for power generation. In addition, it is estimated that the United States has 16,240 square kilometers of roof area and 6,086 square kilometers of building facades that are suitable for installing solar photovoltaics (PVs); mounting solar panels on just half of this area could supply a further 25 percent of U.S. electricity. Additional solar energy can be used to provide water and space heating in buildings, displacing large quantities of natural gas.

Bioenergy, Geothermal Energy, and Ocean Energy

The potential of bioenergy is limited by the availability of fertile land and water, but recent studies indicate that it is larger than most people realize. Today's bioenergy production is based on a combination of food crops (mainly sugarcane and corn) and waste materials from agriculture, forestry, and cities. But the technology is advancing rapidly, dramatically increasing the energy yields per hectare. In the near future, more advanced technologies will allow the conversion of any cellulosic material (such as straw or wood) into liquid biofuels. A joint study by the U.S. Departments of Energy and Agriculture concludes that the nation has enough biomass resources to sustainably meet well over one-third of current U.S. petroleum needs by relying on cellulosic resources and technologies. The legendary Silicon Valley venture capitalist Vinod Khosla, who is investing tens of millions of dollars in bioenergy companies, published an extensive article in the October 2006 issue of *Wired* magazine arguing that new technology will allow advanced biofuels to one day provide all the country's liquid fuel.

Geothermal and ocean energy round out the world's renewable energy portfolio. Although their near-term role is limited by the availability of economical conversion technologies, scores of companies are now developing devices to harness geothermal heat and the energy in the world's waves, tides, and ocean currents. These technologies are just beginning to become competitive, but globally, wave and ocean thermal energy are each estimated to be of the same order of magnitude as present world energy use. The Electric Power Research Institute estimates that U.S. near-shore wave resources could generate 2.3 trillion kWh [kilowatt-hours] of electricity per year, equivalent [to] 60 percent of current U.S. electricity consumption.

The Feasibility of Renewable Energy Increases

Resource availability does not place a practical limit on the potential role of renewable energy, as it does with oil. Rather,

Public Lands and Renewable Energy Development

Our nation's vast and varied lands will play a central role in the transition from fossil fuels to renewable energy and energy efficiency. Since the early 19th century, our public, private, state, and tribal lands have been a vital source of the raw energy inputs that power the country. As we transition to a clean energy economy, these lands will supply the nation with renewable energy from sources such as the sun, wind, and the earth. Along with other land ownership types, public lands will play an important role in these 21st-century solutions to our energy needs. . . .

By working together to strike a balance between ecosystem services and the need for renewable energy, we can protect our valued and unique open spaces and simultaneously meet our energy and climate challenges.

Union of Concerned Scientists,
"Land Conservation and Renewable Energy Development:
Finding a Balance in a Warming World," September 2009.

economics and policy are the two factors that have limited its deployment to date. Although some renewable energy sources, including ethanol and wind power, are already competitive at current energy prices, other renewable technologies are still more expensive than fossil fuels (at least when external economic, social, environmental, and security costs are not accounted for). But this is changing rapidly as technology advances, spurred in part by the kind of double-digit growth rates that dramatically reduced the cost of technologies such as personal computers and mobile phones. A classic study by the Boston Consulting Group found that each time cumulative production of a manufactured device doubles, production costs fall by between 20 and 30 percent. The all-time cumulative production of wind turbines has doubled in the past three-and-a-half years, while cumulative production of solar PVs has doubled in just two-and-a-half years.

Other technical challenges must also be surmounted for large-scale reliance on renewable energy to be feasible. Many renewable resources are intermittent, and while it has been demonstrated that they can provide at least 20 percent of grid electricity without making any major adjustments in the power grid, as their contribution grows, backup or storage capability will have to be added. Fortunately, batteries and other storage technologies are also advancing rapidly, driven (along with renewables) by a surge of venture capital investment. In the long run, hydrogen derived from water through electrolysis will provide a means of storing and transporting energy captured from the full range of renewable resources. Scores of companies are working on fuel cells that efficiently turn hydrogen into electricity to power homes, industries, and motor vehicles.

The Transition to Renewable Energy Is Under Way

Of course, the more quickly energy efficiency advances—and the need for energy supply falls—the greater contribution renewable energy can make. Despite significant improvements in energy efficiency over the past 30-some years, the potential for future savings in the United States and elsewhere remains enormous. Take buildings, which account for more than 40 percent of global energy use. Experts believe that the integration of intelligent design with several efficiency measures could reduce energy use in buildings by 5–80 percent while providing significant economic savings.

It will naturally take time for renewable energy to displace fossil fuels—just as it took decades for oil to replace coal and wood. But this transition is well under way. Global investment in renewable energy has doubled since 2001, and is estimated at $38 billion in 2005. This compares with total investment in the conventional power sector in 2004 of about $150 billion. Riding a surge of new government policies in dozens of countries, capital is flowing into the new technologies—from major corporations such as General Electric, Siemens, and BP [British Petroleum], from large banks such as Goldman Sachs, and from dozens of venture capital firms. Global biofuels production increased 20 percent in 2005, and the production of wind turbines and solar PVs both increased 44 percent. In the last two years, U.S. additions to its wind energy generating capacity exceeded additions to either its coal-fired or nuclear capacity.

The tipping point will come when the world adds enough renewable resources to the energy supply each year that demand for fossil fuels levels off—halting the growth in carbon dioxide emissions. Reaching this point is primarily a matter of political will. We believe that if policy and technology continue to advance at the pace they have in the past five years, that point will be reached 10–15 years from now.

There are no physical or practical limits that would prevent renewable resources from one day providing all of the world's energy. The urgency of the world's energy security and climate problems, and the policies that governments enact to address them, will help determine the pace at which this transition occurs.

> "Solar cells, windmills, and other forms
> of solar flow may be made cheaper . . .
> but land requirements will never be re-
> duced."

Renewable Energy Sources Cannot Meet America's Energy Demands

William Tucker

Renewable energy sources require large tracts of open land on which to construct new energy receptors and generators. In the following viewpoint, William Tucker argues that this fact will eternally limit the volume of energy that renewable sources can produce, thus making these sources incapable of meeting the energy demands of the United States. As Tucker reports, even the high-tech industry of Silicon Valley, which has continually reduced the amount of space needed to store increasing amounts of information, will be unable to decrease the amount of land required for alternate sources to produce significant supplies of power. In addition to the restrictive space constraints, Tucker highlights the relative inefficiency of renewable power sources when compared to traditional energy sources such as gasoline,

William Tucker, "There's Plenty of Energy at the Bottom," *American Spectator*, vol. 42, April 2009, pp. 26–31. Copyright © The American Spectator 2009. Reproduced by permission.

coal, and natural gas. Tucker is a journalist and author who spent the past twenty-five years writing about energy and the environment. He is the author of Terrestrial Energy: How Nuclear Power Will Lead the Green Revolution and End America's Energy Odyssey.

As you read, consider the following questions:

1. Why, according to Tucker, will Silicon Valley be unable to solve the energy crisis using Moore's Law?

2. As reported by the author, what percentage of the sun's rays can be converted into electricity?

3. How much land would the various renewable energy plans cited by the author require?

On December 29, 1959, on the threshold of the 1960s, [American physicist] Richard Feynman, "the best mind since Einstein" and interpreter of quantum mechanics, gave a lecture at the California Institute of Technology that is generally regarded to be the opening bell of the Information Age. It was titled, "There's Plenty of Room at the Bottom."

"There is a device on the market, they tell me, that can write the Lord's Prayer on the head of a pin," Feynman began. "But that's nothing. . . . It is a staggeringly small world below. In the year 2000, when they look back at this age, they will wonder why it was not until the year 1960 that anybody began seriously to move in this direction."

Feynman was talking about the storage of information. The smallest dot in a half-tone photo in the encyclopedia, he noted, if reduced by a factor of 25,000, would still contain in its area 1,000 atoms. Since electron microscopes could already scan pictures this small, why not store information at this level? Switching to the digital language of computers—1s and 0s—only made the possibilities even greater.

Using Less Space to Store More Information

It turns out that all of the information that man has carefully accumulated in all the books in the world can be written in this form in a cube of material one two-hundredth of an inch wide—which is the barest piece of dust that can be made out by the human eye. So there is plenty of room at the bottom! Don't tell me about microfilm!

It wasn't long, of course, before we began to fulfill this vision. In 1965, Gordon Moore, one of the founders of Intel, noted that the number of transistors that could be packed into an integrated circuit was doubling approximately every two years. This principle became "Moore's Law," which still holds to this day. Ultra-dense optical storage disks now hold 120 gigabytes, enough to hold an entire library floor of academic journals. In 2007, the world stored 161 exabytes, enough to pile twelve stacks of books reaching the sun. There is no indication that this revolution is slowing down. As we enter the quantum world, it may become possible to store a 1 or a 0 in the energy state of a single electron. There is still plenty of room at the bottom.

The High-Tech Industry Focuses on Renewable Energy

Spurred by this historical accomplishment, however, Silicon Valley [an area in northern California with a high concentration of high-tech computer companies] has now decided to tackle the energy problem. Energy has become the "next big thing" in the land of information technology, with entrepreneurs who made their fortunes in computers now moving their investments into solar cells, biofuels-improved efficiency, and all forms of "renewable" and "alternate" energy. "My greatest hope is that Silicon Valley will solve the current energy problem with the same genius that it has solved the problems of commercializing the integrated circuit, biotechnology and the Internet," says T. J. Rodgers, founder of Cypress Semiconductor [a company that develops improved technologies for electronic communications devices such as modems], who has now funded SunPower, a photovoltaics start-up [to develop solar panels for energy production]. Legendary Silicon Valley investor John Doerr has hired Nobel Prize winner Al Gore to help select a number of wind and solar start-ups that he calls "cleantech." Adds Vinod Khosla, a co-founder of Sun Microsystems who has become the most active energy venture capitalist in California, "A crisis is a terrible thing to waste."

All this has raised great expectations among alternative energy enthusiasts of a world marriage between environmentalism and high tech. As Fred Krupp, CEO [chief executive officer] of the Environmental Defense Fund, says in his book, *Earth: The Sequel*:

> For investors who made their first fortunes from semiconductors and the Internet, the learning curve on photovoltaics is not terribly steep. Solar power has grown up alongside the chip industry, borrowing its materials and processes and, increasingly, its talent. The geographies of the two industries overlap. Many of the solar start-ups are in California's Silicon Valley, in Cambridge, Massachusetts, in Phoenix, Arizona, and in Austin, Texas. And many have close relations with the same universities: Stanford; University of California, Berkeley; the California Institute of Technology; and MIT [Massachusetts Institute of Technology].

The holy grail of this venture—a new Moore's Law—will be discovered in the field of energy. As reporter G. Pascal Zachary wrote in the *New York Times* in February 2008:

> There is, after all, a precedent for how the [Silicon] Valley tried to approach such tasks, and it's embodied in Moore's Law.... A link between Moore's Law and solar technology reflects the engineering reality that computer chips and solar cells have a lot in common.

Or as Oliver Morton, chief news and features editor of *Nature*, has expressed it, "If Silicon Valley can apply Moore's Law to the capture of sunshine, it could change the world again."

Silicon Valley Will Not Solve the Energy Crisis

Unfortunately, we can say with absolute certainty: "It ain't never gonna happen." There is absolutely no chance that all the money in Silicon Valley is ever going to discover a "Moore's Law" that will allow us to miniaturize the generation of energy the way it has miniaturized the storage of information. Why? The answer is simple: Energy and information are not the same thing.

The marvelous miniaturization embodied in Moore's Law was accomplished by using less and less energy to store each individual bit of information. Think of an abacus. The position of each bead represents a 1 or a 0, and the amount of energy required to move the bead across the wire frame is the cost of storing that information. If we move down into the microcosm so we are storing information by the energy used to change the state of a logic gate or a group of molecules or a single molecule or even a single electron, we are using less and less energy at every level. That is the essence of Moore's Law.

The Limits of Renewable Energy Production

But what if we are seeking to generate energy? We cannot move down the molecular scale in the same way. At each and every stage we will encounter less energy. There is only so much energy stored in a chemical bond or in a flow of photons or electrons. This is easy enough to calculate. The amount of energy stored in a single carbon-hydrogen bond in a fossil fuel is about 1 electron volt (eV). The amount of energy in a

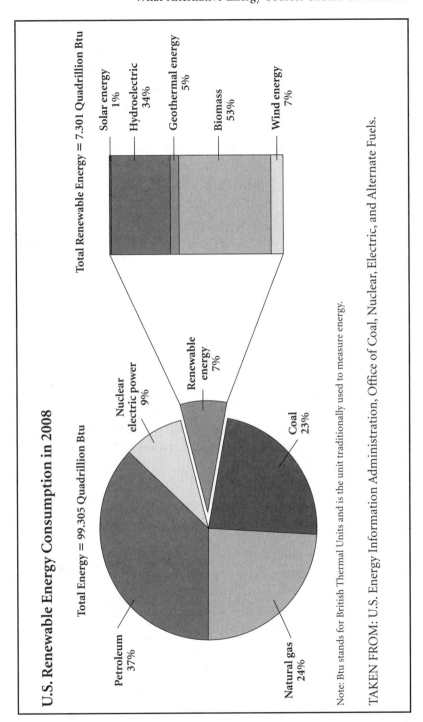

U.S. Renewable Energy Consumption in 2008

Total Energy = 99.305 Quadrillion Btu

Total Renewable Energy = 7.301 Quadrillion Btu

Solar energy
1%

Hydroelectric
34%

Geothermal energy
5%

Biomass
53%

Wind energy
7%

Nuclear electric power
9%

Renewable energy
7%

Coal
23%

Petroleum
37%

Natural gas
24%

Note: Btu stands for British Thermal Units and is the unit traditionally used to measure energy.

TAKEN FROM: U.S. Energy Information Administration, Office of Coal, Nuclear, Electric, and Alternate Fuels.

photon of visible light is in the range of 1.7–3.3 eV. When we break one of those chemical bonds—through the process of "combustion"—or capture a photon in a photovoltaic cell, we can generate about 1 to 3.3 eV of energy.

In fact, we already do a pretty efficient job of capturing and converting these sources of energy. A liter of gasoline, for example, can produce 9.7 kilowatt-hours (kWh) of power—probably the densest form of chemical energy we will ever encounter. Anthracite coal produces 9.4 kWh, liquid natural gas 7.2 kWh, methanol 4.6 kWh, and wood around .5–.9 kWh, depending on its moisture content. "Biofuels"—crops that are less dense and more saturated than wood—produce even fewer kilowatt-hours per liter.

Sunup to sundown, the sun's rays shed about 400 watts per square meter of ground in the United States. By theoretical limits, only about 25 percent of this can be converted into electricity. This means that solar electricity can light one 100-watt bulb for every card table. Covering every square foot of every building in the country with solar panels would be enough to provide our indoor lighting—about 4 percent of our total electrical consumption—during the daytime. Other forms of solar energy flows—wind, hydroelectricity, or biofuels—are more dilute.

The Staggering Land Requirements of Renewable Energy

The only way to make up for the relatively low density of solar flow is to use more land in gathering it. There is no Moore's Law waiting to improve the process. Solar cells, windmills, and other forms of solar flow may be made cheaper—which is where most of the research is going right now—but land requirements will never be reduced. Those requirements, when confronted, turn out to be staggering.

In a 2007 essay that is becoming a classic, Jesse Ausubel, [director] of the Program for the Human Environment at

Rockefeller University [which communicates results of scientific research concerning the environment conducted at the university], calculated the amount of land that would be required to equal the output from fossil fuels using so-called "renewable" energy. Running a 1,000-megawatt [MW] electrical station—the standard size—for example, would require 1,000 square miles of forest. A hydroelectric dam generating 1,000 MW usually backs up a reservoir of about 250 square miles. [Former oilman and current renewable energy advocate] T. Boone Pickens's plan to generate 4,000 MW of electricity from wind in West Texas will cover around 1,200 square miles. In the January 2008 issue of *Scientific American*, three solar energy theorists presented a "grand plan for solar energy" that would involve powering the entire country by covering 30,000 square miles of Southwest desert with solar collectors.

There Will Never Be Enough Land

No amount of technical ingenuity or venture capital flowing out of Silicon Valley is ever going to change these parameters. Cool Earth Solar, for example, a company in Livermore, California, has invented an eight-foot balloon whose surface acts as a magnifying glass to concentrate solar energy on a small photovoltaic cell at its center. This will cut down on the requirements for expensive solar cells. But it will not reduce the space required by the balloons. Bob Metcalfe, co-founder of the Ethernet, is heading GreenFuel Technologies, a Massachusetts company developing photosynthetic algae that will convert the carbon exhausts from a coal plant into biofuel. But the algae pools for a single 1,000-MW coal plant will cover 40 square miles.

Both fossil fuels and solar flows have their limitations. Fossil fuels can produce only so much energy from their chemical bonds. Solar flows can be increased only by covering more land.

Periodical Bibliography

The following articles have been selected to supplement the diverse views presented in this chapter.

Lamar Alexander	"Fission, Baby, Fission! We Need a Hundred New Nuclear Plants," *National Review*, November 2, 2009.
Robert Bryce	"So Much for 'Energy Independence,'" *Wall Street Journal*, July 7, 2009.
Stephen Cass	"Can Renewables Become More than a Sideshow?" *Technology Review*, September/October 2009.
Jonathan Fahey	"Take My Juice," *Forbes*, September 7, 2009.
Christine MacDonald	"Pipe Dreams: The Question of Clean Coal," *E: The Environmental Magazine*, September/October 2009.
Jocelyn Rice	"Putting Clean Coal to the Test," *Discover*, February 2009.
Alexandra Shimo	"A Better Way to Catch Some Sun," *Maclean's*, April 28, 2008.
Rebecca Smith	"The New Nukes," *Wall Street Journal*, September 8, 2009.
Gernot Stoeglehner and Michael Narodoslawsky	"How Sustainable Are Biofuels? Answers and Further Questions Arising from an Ecological Footprint Perspective," *Bioresource Technology*, August 2009.
David Tilman et al.	"Beneficial Biofuels—the Food, Energy, and Environment Trilemma," *Science*, July 17, 2009.

Should Alternatives to Gasoline-Powered Vehicles Be Pursued?

Chapter Preface

In 2008 President Barack Obama offered U.S. automakers $4 billion worth of tax breaks if they helped end America's reliance on foreign oil by retooling their plants to produce more hybrid and environmentally friendly vehicles. So far, the industry leaders have pushed forth a few concept cars and marginally increased their output of consumer hybrid cars. The automakers contend that the demand for these vehicles is just not high enough in the United States to warrant vast and expensive shifts in infrastructure. A sagging economy certainly accounts for slack demand, but consumers also point to the high sticker prices of these cars in comparison to their relatively fuel-efficient, traditional gas-powered counterparts.

Mike Tidwell of the Chesapeake Climate Action Network claims that the "lack of demand" argument is fallacious. He asserts that consumer interest in hybrid and other alternative-fuel vehicles is growing but that the major American auto companies are reluctant to spend money on restructuring when profits can still be made on the gas-powered vehicles that they can easily produce. He told the Cybercast News Service, "Detroit claims that consumers don't want these vehicles, while every day Detroit pays thousands of dollars to lobbyists to stop any kind of passage of higher gas mileage standards that would lead to hybrid cars, while it sues states that try to go on their own [to impose higher gas mileage standards]." Tidwell sees this as a vicious circle that will simply stall production of more environmentally sound and fuel-efficient autos so that U.S. automakers can make more money on existing models.

Lack of demand, though, is not the only thing stalling the production of hybrid vehicles. Several analysts have noted that if hybrid electric cars ever won over a large percentage of the consumer base, then the demand for electricity would rise as owners were forced to recharge their car batteries periodically. The Oak Ridge National Laboratory predicts that by 2030, the prevalence of electric cars could have serious negative consequences for American power usage. "In the worst-case scenario—if all hybrid owners charged their vehicles at 5 P.M., at six kilowatts of power—up to 160 large power plants would be needed nationwide to supply the extra electricity," the lab's researchers claim. Environmentalists have countered this assessment by insisting that the demand for electricity may go up, but its cost and impact will be offset. For instance, the price of powering up a hybrid electric vehicle would compare to paying just $0.75 for a gallon of gas to run a traditional auto, according to a 2007 study by the nonprofit Electric Power Research Institute (EPRI). In addition, the Natural Resources Defense Council, working in tandem with EPRI, expects that any extra electricity needed to power growing numbers of green vehicles will be supplied not by coal-burning power plants but by wind and solar energy producers.

In the following chapter, several experts on both sides of the alternative-fuel debate examine the pros and cons of changing the way America powers the increasing number of automobiles that travel its roadways. Some assert the price—in terms of both dollar amounts and environmental impact—of supposedly clean energy and clean automobile technology is too high, while others argue that the cost of inaction is profoundly higher.

> *"When Americans sit in rush-hour traf-*
> *fic consuming this precious grain in*
> *their SUVs, while others around the*
> *world starve, the corn issue changes*
> *from economical to moral."*

Ethanol Takes Food from the Hungry to Use as Fuel

Donnie Johnston

Donnie Johnston maintains in the following viewpoint that America must make a moral decision about the use of corn to make ethanol. In Johnston's opinion, investing in ethanol production means that America must sacrifice crops that could be used for food for the nation to appear environmentally friendly. Johnston claims this trade-off is absurd; he believes the "green" qualities of ethanol are suspect and that it is far more important to feed the world's starving people than to use corn as an alternative fuel. Johnston warns that if America does not make the right moral choice and disband the use of food crops to make fuel, the world's poor and hungry will rise up and forcefully take what they need to survive. Johnston is a reporter for the Free Lance-Star, *a newspaper in Fredericksburg, Virginia.*

As you read, consider the following questions:

1. What reason does Johnston give to explain why more of the abundant corn crops in America are not sold for food worldwide?

2. Why does Johnston claim that ethanol production may not be saving America from using more oil?

3. According to Johnston, what will the world do when it runs out of oil? What will it do when it runs out of food?

At what point does using corn for fuel become a moral issue?

With an estimated 25 percent of last year's [2007] corn crop being turned into ethanol, some believe we are already there.

The recent two-year rise in gasoline and diesel prices has led to increased pressure for America to produce fuel from something other than oil. Corn, and in a smaller sense soybeans, was seen as the answer.

These are renewable energy sources. The world's oil reserves, once depleted, will be gone. Corn can be grown every year.

The problem is that corn is more than just a grain that can be turned into a means of getting our kids to and from soccer practice.

Corn is a food staple that much of the world depends on, not for entertainment, but for survival. When Americans sit in rush-hour traffic consuming this precious grain in their SUVs [sport-utility vehicles], while others around the world starve, the corn issue changes from economical to moral.

The Rise in Corn Prices

Yes, America grows more corn than our population can eat, and yes, we grow more corn than the world can buy. But we do not grow more corn than the world's population can consume.

Part of the reason that more corn isn't sold for food worldwide is because third world countries cannot afford it. And this problem is getting bigger every day.

In the past three years, corn prices have gone from under $2 a bushel to $6 a bushel. That's a 300 percent increase, comparable to the rise in cost for a barrel of oil over the same period.

Why has this happened? Is the world eating three times as many corn flakes or hush puppies?

Of course not. It is happening because more and more corn is being turned into ethanol in an effort to lower our dependence on foreign oil.

Now cereal makers, corn-syrup manufacturers and other food industries that use vast quantities of corn are competing with ethanol companies for every bushel of corn that is produced.

That means that the price of this golden grain is skyrocketing, as is the cost of related foods. Most Americans are able to cope with these price increases, but people in poorer countries are not. Every time corn goes up even a penny, someone in some poor country will likely go without food.

Suddenly, ethanol becomes a moral issue.

It Takes Oil to Produce Ethanol

When you get right down to it, just how much oil do we save by producing ethanol?

Farmers use diesel trucks to pick up corn seed and deliver the harvested grain. They use diesel tractors to plow the fields, plant the corn and fertilize it. Trucks or tractors are used to spray pesticides on the land and gasoline pumps irrigate fields to achieve greater productivity.

Most commercial fertilizers applied to the land are oil-based and combines [harvesters] burn gallons of diesel (or ethanol) when grain is harvested.

Ethanol Production Is Raising the Price of Corn

On Apr. 10 [2009] the Congressional Budget Office [CBO] published a report saying that "higher use of the corn-based fuel additive [ethanol] accounted for about 10% to 15% of the rise in food prices between April 2007 and April 2008." That's just for one year.

Ethanol use has much more impact on prices of foods directly connected to corn, whether it be Kellogg's Corn Flakes or beef from the butcher's department at your local grocery store. An especially alarming CBO statistic shows another hidden cost of ethanol: Increased food prices could cost Americans $900 million more for food stamps and nutritional programs for children.

Ed Wallace, "The Ethanol Lobby: Profits vs. Food," BusinessWeek, *May 26, 2009.*

Ethanol plants also use electricity, and generating electricity means using oil somewhere along the line.

One study says that ethanol, when combined with gasoline, can save maybe 40 cents a gallon. Given the above, I seriously doubt that.

But, ethanol is politically correct and we live in a politically correct society. If third world children starve so we can call ourselves "green," then so be it.

Our insatiable thirst for fuel has already led us into a war in the Middle East. The world is not enamored with that.

Now we are using precious grain to satisfy that thirst even more, and in doing so, we are driving food prices so high that more and more of the world's population is going hungry. That certainly isn't going to win us any Brownie points.

Suddenly, oil and corn are inextricably linked, and a war for one may soon be a war for the other.

Making a Moral Decision

We talk "global" but we think national. In American terms, "global" means "anything we can take from the rest of the world." And we believe we have the right to take it.

But are we right in this belief? Are we morally correct to force others to go hungry so we can mow 3-acre lawns?

Some congressmen—including Senator John McCain, the presumptive Republican presidential nominee [in 2008]—are now questioning the Environmental Protection Agency's mandate that America produce five times as much ethanol by 2022 as it will this year. These lawmakers have made those concerns known in an open letter to the federal agency.

When the oil runs out, society, as it always has, will adapt. When the food runs out, however, the world will riot.

And if we are the only country left with food, the rest of the world will kill us to get it. That's not terrorism; that's self-preservation.

Food for the masses or fuel for the privileged few? That's the crossroads at which we are now standing, and it is time for a moral—not a reality—check before we press on.

Remember, too, that history has proven that the most dangerous people are those who are starving and have nothing to lose.

We live in complicated times.

"Far from starving the world's poor . . .
biofuels can help the world meet its energy needs without jeopardizing food
security."

Ethanol Does Not Use Food for Fuel

Tom Daschle

*Tom Daschle is a Democrat and a former U.S. senator from
South Dakota. In the following viewpoint, Daschle argues against
critics of ethanol production on the grounds that it will deplete
food stocks. Daschle maintains that only 5 percent of the U.S.
corn crop is used to feed people and that any reduction of the remaining 95 percent to make ethanol will quickly be made up by
farmers simply growing more corn to meet the increased demand. Daschle states that many countries are already investing
in biofuel technology and that America will be forced to follow
suit as carbon-based energy costs rise.*

As you read, consider the following questions:

1. When does Daschle predict the United States will embrace a cap-and-trade emissions program?

Tom Daschle, C. Ford Runge, and Benjamin Senauer, "Food for Fuel?" *Foreign Affairs*,
vol. 86, September/October 2007, pp. 157–62. Copyright © 2007 by the Council on Foreign Relations, Inc. Reproduced by permission of the publisher, www.foreignaffairs.org.

2. By how many bushels of harvested corn did U.S. production increase between 1980 and 2006, according to
Daschle?

3. Daschle reports that 5 percent of the U.S. corn crop is
used to feed people. For what, does he say, is the other
95 percent used?

The [*Foreign Affairs*] article "How Biofuels Could Starve
the Poor," by C. Ford Runge and Benjamin Senauer (May/
June 2007), recycles the "food versus fuel" mythology that has
been rebutted time and again. Despite the authors' allegations,
the facts are clear: U.S. corn is used to feed mostly animals,
not people; converting the starch from a portion of the U.S.
corn crop into biofuels is an efficient way to reduce the United
States' dangerous dependence on imported oil; and the recent
firming of grain prices in the United States—and therefore the
world—will help, not hurt, farmers in food-deficit nations.
Most important, current production facilities for grain-based
biofuels are a critical platform for launching the next generation of advanced cellulosic and waste-derived biofuel technologies.

To their credit, Runge and Senauer recognize that ending
the United States' suicidal dependence on fossil fuels will require a comprehensive energy policy. They are absolutely right:
Any solution to the world's twin energy and climate crises will
need to be broad and multifaceted. Existing energy sources
must be used more efficiently through increased fuel-efficiency
requirements, better building codes and appliance standards,
and market-driven demand-side management programs, such
as ones that give utility companies profit incentives to increase
energy efficiency and conservation. The playing field for renewable sources of energy—such as wind, solar, and geothermal energy—must be leveled with tax incentives that reduce
the production costs for renewable-energy technologies. And
the increasingly perilous costs of climate change (which is

caused by the unbridled use of fossil fuels) must be stemmed with a binding international regulatory framework for greenhouse gases that includes the United States and China, the world's largest emitters of such gases today.

Benefits of Biofuels

Unfortunately, Runge and Senauer distort the central role that biofuels will play in any such comprehensive solution, both in the United States and abroad. Far from starving the world's poor, as they claim, biofuels can help the world meet its energy needs without jeopardizing food security.

The current generation of biofuels has significant environmental benefits. The U.S. federal policy that requires minimum levels of oxygenates in U.S. gasoline has improved air quality in the United States while increasing the use of biofuels—two of the primary benefits that Senator Bob Dole and I sought when we successfully pushed for that policy in 1991. The current generation of biofuels also helps reduce the emission of greenhouse gases. An interesting analysis released by the Natural Resources Defense Council last May [2007] showed that corn-based ethanol outperforms gasoline when the two fuels' full production and use cycles are compared. Innovation in the biofuel industry is leading to even greater greenhouse gas reductions, regardless of the feedstock.

Runge and Senauer themselves argue that the next generation of biofuels will dramatically lessen greenhouse gases. But not content to highlight these benefits, the authors stack the deck by focusing on the costs of developing these fuels. The problem is that their cost predictions take no account of the effects of innovation or of policy proposals that appear likely to be implemented over the next several years (and which they support).

Starting a Tidal Wave of Change

One such proposal is for a U.S.-wide carbon cap-and-trade system, which would immediately provide an economic advantage to fuels with lower carbon content. Although such a system is unlikely to come into being under the current president [George W. Bush], most analysts believe that it will by 2012. Another significant proposal is for new state and federal incentives for low-carbon fuels, such as the program now being implemented in California, which is set to take full effect by November 2008. By mandating that a growing percentage of the market for transportation fuel be set aside for low-carbon fuels, such programs would unleash a tidal wave of private-sector investment and technological innovation that would ultimately bring about something of a low-carbon-fuel Manhattan Project [a program dedicated to developing the first atomic bomb during World War II]. In stark contrast to the head-in-the-sand policies of the Bush administration, the example of these policies could serve as a beacon to the rest of the world and encourage similar behavior elsewhere, including in China and India.

Under either of these policies, both the costs associated with carbon-intensive fossil fuels and the incentives for innovation in low-carbon fuels would dramatically increase. Thus, it is reasonable to expect cellulose-based ethanol to be competitive far sooner than in ten years, the time frame predicted by Runge and Senauer.

No Food Crunch in the Future

Having lived through three decades of debates about ethanol, I can attest that the critics of biofuels have often warned of a coming food crunch as a result of the competition for inputs needed to produce both food and fuel. One of the most memorable such predictions arose in 1980, during my second term in Congress, in the form of a Worldwatch Institute pamphlet entitled *Food or Fuel: New Competition for the World's Cropland*. I was among those who rebutted the argument, which was authored by Lester [R.] Brown, and predicted that U.S. farmers and technology would more than keep pace with demand not only for food and feed but also for fuel. Over the next several decades, the doomsayers were proved wrong: Productivity gains for corn averaged nearly three percent per year, and the annual U.S. corn crop increased from approximately seven billion bushels in 1980 to nearly 12 billion bushels in 2006. During most of that time, corn prices were far below the actual costs of corn production, and taxpayers spent billions in direct payments to farmers in order to maintain the nation's "cheap food" policy. Last year [2006], the Worldwatch Institute released a report warning of the potential effect of biofuels on food but highlighting, above all, their benefits for farmers and the climate.

In August 2005, President George W. Bush signed the Renewable Fuel Standard Program into law, and U.S. ethanol production is now expected to approach eight billion gallons by next year. As the public's attention has begun to focus on the need for alternatives to oil, the major oil companies have become concerned. Unsurprisingly, warnings of a looming food-fuel trade-off have crept back into the national debate.

Yet I am convinced that just as the crunch never came during the past 25-plus years, it will not come now.

Higher Corn Prices Will Not Be Passed on to Consumers

A recent analysis of the Bureau of Labor Statistics' food pricing data by the National Corn Growers Association showed that annual inflation for a basket of corn-intensive foodstuffs, such as dairy products, chicken, and pork, was less than general annual food inflation. And so even though the price of yellow corn in the United States has gone from $1.98 per bushel in January 2006 to $3.76 per bushel in March 2007, the increase has not been passed on to U.S. consumers of products such as milk, cheese, chicken, and pork.

There are a number of possible reasons for this (none of which Runge and Senauer cite). One of them is that only

The Real Culprits Behind Hikes in Food Prices

Watching the news and listening to some of my colleagues [in the U.S. Senate], I've heard the domestic ethanol industry being blamed for price hikes and shortages of apples, broccoli, rice, wheat, lentils, peppers and even bananas. With regard to wheat, rice and lentils, the global demand for food from a growing middle class in China and India has the most impact. Weather trends including a drought in Australia and poor growing conditions in Southeast Asia and Eastern Europe have had a much greater impact on the supply of rice and wheat. Many of these countries also have government production policies that manipulate the production, supply and trading of these commodities. The fact is, the global demand and price for all commodities has increased. Some of this could be due to speculation. But, the biggest culprit behind the rising food costs is $125 a barrel oil.

Chuck Grassley,
"Ethanol Is Not the Cause of All That Ails You,"
prepared statement for U.S. Senate, May 15, 2008.

about five percent of the U.S. corn crop is used directly for human food; much of the remaining 95 percent is used to feed livestock. Another reason is that ruminant animals, such as beef and dairy cattle, get more nutritional value out of feed made from ethanol coproducts than out of other feed. The benefits are less great for monogastric animals, such as swine and poultry, but the market can still get the most bang for the bushel by converting the starch in corn into ethanol and then using the protein coproducts from ethanol plants for ruminants' feed rations.

To be sure, short-term market gyrations will require adjustments, as was the case in response to the recent hikes in prices for tortilla flour in Mexico cited by the authors. But this will be a short-lived challenge because the market will rapidly respond to the increased demand for corn by encouraging farmers to plant more of it. The U.S. Department of Agriculture estimates that there will be as many as 90 million acres of corn planted this year in the United States and tens of millions of acres more planted in South America and elsewhere. If history is any indication, productivity per acre will increase year after year as technology improves the characteristics of seeds, including their starch content and ability to ferment. And in the medium term, of course, feedstocks other than corn, including non-food cellulose, will become increasingly important as inputs for biofuels.

Overcoming Fears and Doomsday Predictions

The legislation promoting a low-carbon fuel standard now being considered by Congress will attract investment for next-generation facilities that convert animal waste and other waste (replacing fossil fuel inputs) into biogas and biofertilizers. As energy costs rise, farmers will increasingly rely on low- and no-till cultivation techniques. And as their incomes improve, they will have more capital available to employ other environmentally friendly techniques. An acre of corn, one of the rare plant species to use a carbon-dioxide-efficient photosynthesis system, removes more carbon dioxide from the atmosphere than does an acre of mature Amazonian rain forest, and next-generation biofuel technologies—including those using non-food cellulosic feedstocks—will increasingly contribute to the critically important goal of reducing, as the author Michael Pollan has put it, humans' "carbon footprint."

Next-generation feedstocks in other countries will also be important. Runge and Senauer sound the alarm about the potential use of cassava—an important foodstuff—for biodiesel, but cassava is far from being the most promising feedstock for biodiesel in developing countries. In fact, oil from jatropha, a non-food plant that grows in wastelands, is widely used in India, where it is the main ingredient in the 15–20 percent biodiesel fuel that powers the trains running from New Delhi to Mumbai. According to the Energy and Resources Institute in New Delhi, a hectare of jatropha can produce four times as much fuel as a hectare of soybeans. Other countries, such as the Dominican Republic, Haiti, and several African states, have begun to sow jatropha for future use in biodiesel.

Like at no other time in history, the planet faces energy and climate crises. Resolving them will require a comprehensive and well-reasoned set of policies. Those choices must be based on sound analysis—not hyperbole and the hollow recitation of discredited doomsday prophecies.

> *"As more people become environmentally conscious and realize that biodiesel's low sulfur content means there is less soot and cleaner air, they'll make the switch."*

Biodiesel Will Reduce Oil Dependence and Greenhouse Gas Emissions

Fuel Oil News

Fuel Oil News is a magazine that covers all aspects of the oil/petroleum industry by addressing areas of concern in home heating, diesel, and alternative fuels. In the following viewpoint, the magazine argues that biodiesel is an environmentally friendly alternative fuel that has prospect in the home heating industry. Since biodiesel can be made from any fat or vegetable oil and used as fuel for heating or transportation, it can reduce America's dependence on oil. The article also argues that because biodiesel has low sulfur content, it releases less greenhouse gas emissions and helps keep the air cleaner.

As you read, consider the following questions:

1. According to the viewpoint, how many gallons of heating oil could be conserved if everyone in the Northeast used a B5 blend in an oil furnace?

2. As stated in the viewpoint, since 2003, how many gallons of B20 biodiesel has REC Fleet Fuel Services sold to customers?

3. Does the use of biodiesel fuel require any engine modification?

With winter weather blanketing much of the country, more people began realizing that cleaner burning biodiesel can be used to power their oil furnaces and boilers, significantly lowering emissions. By using an American-made fuel, heating oil companies are working to extend the oil supply and reduce U.S. dependence on foreign sources of oil.

Biodiesel can be made from any fat or vegetable oil, such as soybean oil, and can be used as a heating or transportation fuel. Biodiesel can be introduced into the heating oil pool with few or no modifications to the furnace or boiler and can even help keep it cleaner. Biodiesel can be blended with regular No. 2 heating oil at any level, but a blend of 20 percent biodiesel and 80 percent regular heating oil (B20) is most common.

"I believe one of the most promising markets for biodiesel is the heating oil market" said Joe Jobe, executive director of the National Biodiesel Board. "Research shows that biodiesel can be a viable, immediate part of the solution to high heating oil bills because it can help extend the supply of heating oil. It has many additional benefits as well, such as being a renewable resource, helping to protect the environment, keeping equipment cleaner and reducing our dependence on foreign sources of oil."

Based on 2000 Energy Information Administration data, No. 2 heating oil is consumed in 7.7 million homes in the United States, 5.3 million (69 percent) of them in the Northeast. Residential consumption was 6.7 billion gallons, 5.5 billion (89 percent) of them in the mid-Atlantic and northeastern states. Officials at the United States Department of Agriculture's Beltsville Agricultural Research Center, which has successfully heated its buildings with biodiesel since 2000, estimate that if everyone in the Northeast with an oil furnace used a B5 blend, 50 million gallons of regular heating oil could be conserved. . . .

Future Plans

A number of energy retailers in northeastern and mid-Atlantic states are offering, or have plans to offer, biodiesel for home heating. They include:

Alliance Energy Services. This Holyoke, Mass.-based company began offering B20 to residential customers in western Massachusetts this year [2004]. President Stephen Chase sees a "tremendous future for biodiesel in the heating oil market." He predicts that as more people become environmentally conscious and realize that biodiesel's low sulfur content means there is less soot and cleaner air, they'll make the switch. . . .

Roy Brothers Oil [and Propane]. Marc Bingham, president of Roy Brothers Oil and Propane, a full-service energy retailer in Ashburnham, Mass., also predicts a bright future for biodiesel.

"The potential benefits of biodiesel are far-reaching," said Bingham. "Renewable energy sources, such as biodiesel, can help our country reduce its dependence on foreign sources of oil and at the same time are good for American farmers and the environment." . . .

Vermont's Alternative Energy Corporation. Located in Williston, Vt., Vermont's Alternative Energy Corporation [VAEC] will soon be offering biodiesel for home heating to

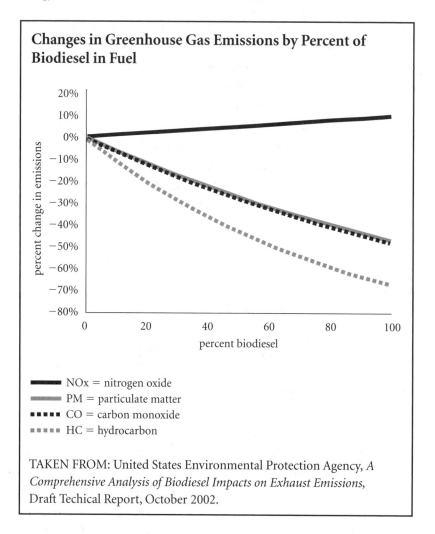

Changes in Greenhouse Gas Emissions by Percent of Biodiesel in Fuel

NOx = nitrogen oxide
PM = particulate matter
CO = carbon monoxide
HC = hydrocarbon

TAKEN FROM: United States Environmental Protection Agency, *A Comprehensive Analysis of Biodiesel Impacts on Exhaust Emissions,* Draft Techical Report, October 2002.

residential customers in the state. In September 2003, VAEC was awarded a grant from the Department of Agriculture to take "Steps Towards a Biorefinery Industry in Vermont."

VAEC proposed a feasibility study to define the best processes in Vermont to produce products necessary for the support of farmers, producers, and users of biorenewables. Included in the study is research for converting farm waste to fuel and compost material. It will also examine oil seed crops suitable for production in the northeastern United States to feed a biorefinery. Finally, it will define biorefinery products that complement local biomass streams (especially waste) and have profit potential to support the biodiesl production process.

So Far, So Good

After six months, Bio-Blend diesel fuel has lived up to expectations.

Last August, and reported in these pages in October 2003, REC Fleet Fuel Services opened Rhode Island's first Bio-Blend diesel fuel island in Providence. After one of the coldest winters in 20 years, according to REC general manager Wendy Hawkins, "the results are astonishing. B20 Bio-Blend diesel does hold up in cold weather temperatures."

Since August 2003, REC has sold over 20,000 gallons of B20 Bio-Blend to customers such as:

- Narragansett Electric Company, which uses the fuel 24/7 in its emergency vehicles.

- CleanScape, Inc., a recycling and landscaping company that uses the fuel in its recycling vehicles.

- Providence Head Start, which uses the B20 in two of its full-size school buses.

Hawkins has monitored the Bio-Blend diesel very carefully throughout this winter to make sure it will perform in cold temperatures. After approximately six months, Hawkins sent a survey to all Bio-Blend diesel users for some feedback on what they thought of the product. Here's what the results of the study have revealed:

- No reported problems with starting vehicles.

- No fuel filter problems.

- Cold weather performance was rated "Good."

- No noticeable change in mileage.

- No more headaches from being around the fuel when a driver is in the truck compartment.

- Many said it smells and performs better than the conventional fuel (petroleum diesel).

REC still sells and monitors the Bio-Blend diesel and needs more participants to use it, so it can be a sustainable source of energy. Biodiesel is safer for "people to breathe," said Curt Gower, owner of REC.

Biodiesel has decreased levels of potential cancer-causing compounds, such as polycyclic aromatic hydrocarbons and nitrated PAH compounds. Biodiesel also reduces dependence on foreign oil and helps support domestic farmers. Many fleet managers have decided that biodiesel is their best cost strategy for complying with state and federal regulations, because there is no engine modification needed to use this fuel. All in all, it is a win-win situation.

> *"If all the kitchen grease in all the world's McDonald's restaurants were converted to biodiesel, it would amount to 75,000 barrels per day, or approximately .004 percent of America's daily oil consumption."*

Biodiesel Will Not Significantly Reduce Oil Dependence

Max Schulz

In the viewpoint that follows, Max Schulz argues that investment in biodiesel is wrongheaded. Schulz claims that conversion to biodiesel is an expensive undertaking, one that has doomed at least one major biodiesel corporation that found that the price of making biofuel was higher than the cost it could charge customers. More importantly, Schulz contends that America does not possess enough used cooking oils or other convertible wastes to make sufficient quantities of biodiesel to wean the country off foreign oil. Schulz is a fellow at the Manhattan Institute's Center for Energy Policy and the Environment, a research organization that promotes market-oriented solutions to economic and social issues.

Max Schulz, "Bio-Fools," *American Spectator*, vol. 42, March 2009, pp. 38–40. Copyright © The American Spectator 2009. Reproduced by permission.

As you read, consider the following questions:

1. How much does a Greasecar conversion kit cost, according to Schulz? Why does he question the economics of such conversions to diesel engines?

2. As Schulz reports, what problems did California governor Arnold Schwarzenegger face when he announced he was running his Hummer on used cooking grease?

3. How much money did Earth Biofuels Inc. lose in 2006 after discovering that its biodiesel production costs were higher than its selling prices?

At a time when sky-high gasoline prices are still a sharp memory, and politicians of all stripes think we need to end our supposed addiction to oil, alternative energy advocates are casting about for something—anything—to use instead of petroleum products, and much of the focus has turned to biofuels.

Corn and cellulosic-based ethanol are most frequently mentioned, and the federal government is spending a lot of money trying to find economical ways to derive this fuel from corncobs and switchgrass stalks. Whatever its merits, ethanol is unquestionably boring. A far more exciting biofuel candidate . . . is biodiesel. Animal and vegetable fat contains triglycerides that, with minimal effort, can be turned into diesel. And conventional diesel engines can be converted to run on a variety of biodiesel products. Unsurprisingly, the most enthusiastic biodiesel advocates come from the environmental movement.

As William Tucker notes in his excellent new book, *Terrestrial Energy[: How Nuclear Power Will Lead the Green Revolution and End America's Energy Odyssey]*, greens have proposed tapping all kinds of sources—cooking grease, food scraps, crop wastes, anything organic—to promote the promise of biodiesel. . . . Writes Tucker, "Typically, someone will design a car that runs on some organic waste—turkey droppings, hayseed, coconut oil—and drive it around until it attracts press attention. Then they will announce they have solved the world's energy problems."

It's the ultimate in recycling. Who hasn't seen a local news report about the enterprising driver who has converted the engine in his car to run on cooking grease he takes off the hands of the local fast-food joint? Sure, the car may smell faintly like fries or Chinese food or whatever the grease was used to cook. The upside to that odor is it will usually mask the scent of patchouli.

Half-Baked Ideas Brought to the Mainstream

For those who think turkey droppings or French fry grease are the path to energy independence, a whole industry has sprung up to help patriotic and environmentally minded drivers make the switch.

Massachusetts-based Greasecar Vegetable Fuel Systems is among the leaders in the car conversion field. Greasecar offers a network of about 40 locations nationwide where installers will retrofit your diesel engine to handle biodiesel. The cost ranges from about $2,000–$3,000 for the kit and installation. Whether this was worth the effort last year [2008], when a gallon of diesel fetched nearly five dollars, isn't clear; it would have taken driving a lot of miles to recoup the investment. Now that the price of diesel is half what it was last summer, the half-baked idea seems to make half as much sense.

Still, it's not just the half-baked crowd that's been showing interest in fueling up on McDonald's discarded fry grease. Switching the old VW [Volkswagen] bus to run on waste vegetable oil used to be the strict preserve of hippies living off the grid and under the radar. But with the spike in pump prices in recent years, a somewhat more respectable clientele—like celebrated Beverly Hills liposuctionists—has emerged as a potential market for diesel engine conversions.

Taking the idea mainstream has brought its share of problems, though. The *Los Angeles Times* profiled a mechanic last year who has converted his fleet of vehicles to be fueled by fryer grease from a local chowder house. Then Sacramento [California's capital] called, not to praise him for his green efforts but to bust him. Apparently he had failed to get his state "diesel fuel supplier's license" and wasn't paying the required 18-cent per gallon tax on the fuel he burned. Oh, and he faced further trouble from California's Meat and Poultry Inspection Branch for removing grease without a license. Then there was his missing permit from the Air Resources Board allowing him to burn fat, not to mention that he didn't have liability insurance to cover potential spills.

Don't just pity the poor mechanic. The state's green governor, Arnold Schwarzenegger, faced a similar conundrum. Trying to set a good eco-example, the Governator has made a point of powering his Hummer on cooking oil from Costco. He wasn't paying taxes or complying with the regs [regulations] either. Several states exempt small-time drivers who run on kitchen grease from paying taxes, as well as from needing to jump through the regulatory hoops that were designed to apply to large-haul handlers of fuel or animal by-products. Given California's budget fiasco (the governor has asked Washington for its own bailout), it's unlikely Sacramento will loosen its requirements anytime soon. Despite this hurdle (the largest concentration of biodiesel vehicles are thought to be in California), biodiesel advocates believe they are making significant inroads into the culture at large.

A Costly Folly

Ironically, the effort to broaden biofuel's image from hippies to a wider segment of the public has employed one of America's best-known long-haired dope smokers as its spokes-

The High Costs of Biodiesel

Despite the green hype, a complicated brew of factors has forced . . . at least a third of America's biodiesel refiners to cease operation. Commodity prices skyrocketed; diesel fell. The credit crisis turned off the cash spigot. Concerns arose about biofuels' impact on South American forests. . . .

The numbers say it all: Last week [in early June 2009], the price of West Coast canola-based biodiesel was about $3.42 per gallon, before taxes; conventional diesel went for under $2. Even with a $1 per gallon federal credit for blenders, biodiesel costs 20 percent more.

John Miller, "Biodiesel Refiners See Red, Not Green,"
Spokesman-Review *(Spokane, WA), June 14, 2009.*

man. In 2005, country music legend Willie Nelson lent his name and image to a product called BioWillie diesel fuel. The Red Headed Stranger has long toured in a biodiesel-powered bus, so his sponsorship seemed natural.

BioWillie was pitched to independent truckers thought to be fed up with paying huge sums to Middle Eastern sheiks when they just as easily could be filling the pockets of American farmers. The idea, as Willie put it, was to "put five million farmers back on the land growing fuel and keep us from having to start wars for oil."

Willie Nelson is certainly a great musician and songwriter, but he has never shown much aptitude for handling women (married four times) or money (his assets were seized in 1990 when the IRS [Internal Revenue Service] said he owed about $17 million in back taxes). So perhaps it's no surprise that BioWillie went belly up. In 2006, Earth Biofuels Inc., the company behind BioWillie, found itself paying more to produce a gallon of biodiesel than it was earning by selling it, hardly a sustainable business practice. Most of the outlets that carried it stopped doing so. Earth Biofuels reportedly lost $63 million in 2006, and Nelson himself quit the board of directors and gave up six million shares of worthless Earth Biofuels stock. The company retains the rights to the BioWillie brand and is continuing feeble efforts to make a go with it.

Not that Willie is dissuaded. He is still a true believer, in 2007 publishing the page-turner *On the Clean Road Again: Biodiesel and the Future of the Family Farm.* It's worth buying, if only for the chapter entitled "To All the Oils I've Loved Before."

For all his goofiness and wrongheadedness on everything from biofuels boosterism to 9/11 [2001 terrorist attacks] conspiracies, Willie Nelson is still the man who penned "Crazy" and "Hello, Walls." He's a national treasure. He puts on a helluva concert, even for a septuagenarian in a perpetual cannabis fog. In my book, Willie Nelson will always get a pass.

Not Enough Food Oil to Replace Crude Oil

Someone who doesn't get a pass, however, is loathsome former Long Island congressman Vito Fossella. Before his career [in the U.S. House of Representatives] was ruined by a DUI [driving under the influence violation] and revelations that he fathered a child with his mistress, Fossella stumped for legislation to double the federal tax credit for using restaurant grease as fuel: "From cooking fried calamari to powering trucks," he announced, "restaurant grease represents a viable energy source for our nation."

Except it doesn't, not by a long shot. As *Terrestrial Energy* points out, if all the kitchen grease in all the world's McDonald's restaurants were converted to biodiesel, it would amount to 75,000 barrels per day, or approximately .004 percent of America's daily oil consumption. According to the Environmental Protection Agency, all U.S. restaurants produce 300 million gallons of waste oil per year. That's about one gallon for every American.

That's not enough to make any sort of dent in our oil consumption, but it does give us incentive to eat more unhealthy fast food. And if that conundrum gives the Left fits, it's good enough for me.

Periodical Bibliography

The following articles have been selected to supplement the diverse views presented in this chapter.

David Boddiger   "Boosting Biofuel Crops Could Threaten Food Security," *Lancet*, September 15, 2007.

Susan Cosier   "Charge!" *Audubon*, September/October 2009.

Alec Dubro   "The Myth of the Efficient Car," *Progressive*, May 2009.

Ecologist   "The Environmental Crop?" March 2007.

Jesse Finfrock and Nichole Wong   "Pouring Biofuel on the Fire," *Mother Jones*, March/April 2009.

Moira Herbst   "The Electric Car Market: Not Fully Charged," *BusinessWeek*, September 17, 2009. www.businessweek.com.

Margaret Kriz   "Is Ethanol Really the Culprit?" *National Journal*, June 7, 2008.

Reed McManus   "Biofuel Takes a Beating," *Sierra*, September/October 2008.

Sunita Satyapal, John Petrovic, and George Thomas   "Gassing up with Hydrogen," *Scientific American*, April 2007.

Robert F. Service   "Hydrogen Cars: Fad or the Future?" *Science*, June 5, 2009.

What Should Be the Government's Role in Advancing Alternative Energy?

Chapter Preface

In February 2009, Max Schulz, a senior fellow at the Manhattan Institute's Center for Energy Policy and the Environment, penned an editorial column in the *Wall Street Journal* criticizing government subsidies of alternative energies. Citing statistics from the U.S. Energy Information Administration, Schulz reported that the government subsidizes solar energy at $24.34 per megawatt-hour (MWh) and wind power at $23.37 per MWh, while subsidizing natural gas at only 25 cents per MWh, coal at 44 cents, hydroelectricity at 67 cents, and nuclear power at a comparatively high $1.59. Schulz notes that presently alternative energies provide less than 1 percent of America's electrical energy needs, leaving the preponderance of electricity production to those resources that have consistently been able to meet the growing demand for power.

President Barack Obama wants to alter this imbalance by committing America to an energy plan that will ensure that the nation will receive 25 percent of its energy needs from alternative sources by 2025. In Schulz's opinion, however, forcing America to increase clean electrical energy resources is wrongheaded. As Schulz contends, alternative energy technologies are "big losers" from an economic perspective, which is why the government has to subsidize them so heavily. Making these resources responsible for more energy production will simply mean that their high expense will be passed on to more consumers as will the price of the backup energy needed to supplant the wind and solar power on cloudy days or days with no breeze.

Not everyone sees the discrepancy in energy subsidies the same way, though. Jay Yarow, a journalist who covers technology and media for the *Business Insider*, believes that if the intention of the government is to create an energy system that reduces fossil fuel consumption and carbon dioxide emissions, then it would be more appropriate to compare subsidies of alternative energy resources (which, in his tally, includes hydropower, wind, solar, and geothermal energies) against the total subsidies of all fossil fuel sources. Thus, even if renewable resources receive the greater share of subsidies (roughly $4.9 billion in 2007) relative to individual fossil fuel resources and nuclear power, the total subsidies attached to coal, gas, and nuclear power combined is much higher (about $7.2 billion in 2007). Furthermore, Yarow claims that government subsidies have often attended the inception of major industries. He writes that government funded the formative expansion of the Internet, and only after such aid did private investment take over and propel its explosive growth. In Yarow's view, alternative energy technologies will likely follow a similar trajectory that will relieve taxpayers and consumers from bearing the burden of the fledgling industry for long.

In the following chapter, analysts and critics debate government involvement in promoting and subsidizing alternative energies. Some argue that the dream of fossil fuel independence cannot be achieved without government support for alternative energies. Others believe that government should have no part in directing or funding private industry and that such participation will end up costing the American taxpayers too much.

| *"Because the payoffs from research in transformational technologies are both higher risk and longer term, government investment is critical and appropriate."*

Government Investment Is Necessary to Further Develop Alternative Energy

Steven Chu

Much of the debate concerning the proliferation of alternative energy technologies centers on cost and technological advancement. In the following viewpoint, Steven Chu, secretary of the U.S. Department of Energy (DOE), argues that government investment in research and development of energy alternatives is necessary to make these technologies competitive with other energy sources such as petroleum and coal. Chu asserts that legislation passed to spur economic recovery in response to the recent recession includes important provisions that will provide incentives for corporations and individuals to begin drawing energy from alternative sources and improving energy efficiency. In addition to government incentives, Secretary Chu emphasizes the

Steven Chu, statement before the Committee on Science and Technology, U.S. House of Representatives, Washington, DC, March 17, 2009. www.energy.gov. Reproduced by permission.

importance of cooperation between the DOE and private compa-nies in decreasing U.S. dependence on foreign oil supplies. Presi-dent Barack Obama appointed Steven Chu the secretary of the DOE in January 2009; Chu won the Nobel Prize in Physics in 1997.

As you read, consider the following questions:

1. As reported by Chu, how will the American Recovery and Reinvestment Act help the United States advance toward a clean energy economy?

2. What steps does Chu suggest be taken to ensure new breakthroughs on energy?

3. In what fields does Chu believe the DOE should con-duct more transformational research?

Today, we import roughly 60 percent of our oil, draining resources from our economy and leaving it vulnerable to supply disruptions. Much of that oil is controlled by regimes that do not share our values, weakening our security. Addi-tionally, if we continue our current rates of greenhouse gas emissions, the consequences for our climate could be disas-trous.

If we, our children, and our grandchildren are to prosper in the 21st century, we must decrease our dependence on oil, use energy in the most efficient ways possible, and lower our carbon emissions. Meeting these challenges will require both swift action in the near term and a sustained commitment for the long term to build a new economy, powered by clean, reli-able, affordable, and secure energy.

During his recent [2009] address to a joint session of Congress, President [Barack] Obama reiterated his commit-ment to reducing our dependence on oil and sharply cutting greenhouse gas emissions. I look forward to working with others in the administration and with members of Congress to meet the president's goal of legislation that places a market-based cap on carbon pollution and drives the production of more renewable energy in America. Such legislation will provide the framework for transforming our energy system to make our economy less carbon-intensive, and less dependent on foreign oil.

The American Recovery and Reinvestment Act and Clean Energy

In the near term, President Obama and this Congress have already taken a key step by passing the American Recovery and Reinvestment Act of 2009. This legislation will put Americans back to work while laying the groundwork for a clean energy economy.

I would like to highlight a few of the energy investments in that law.

First, the Recovery Act will put people to work making our homes and offices more energy efficient. It includes $5 billion to weatherize the homes of low-income families; a $1,500 tax credit to help homeowners invest in efficiency upgrades; $4.5 billion to "green" [make more environmentally friendly] federal buildings, including reducing their energy consumption; and $6.3 billion to implement state and local efficiency and renewable programs.

The Recovery Act also includes $6 billion for loan guarantees and more than $13 billion in tax credits and financial assistance instruments (grants and cooperative agreements) that may leverage tens of billions in private sector investment in clean energy and job creation. This will help clean energy businesses and projects to get off the ground, even in these difficult economic times. The bill also makes investments in key technologies, such as $2 billion in advanced battery manufacturing, and $4.5 billion to jump-start our efforts to modernize the electric grid. These funds will help us ensure that the research investments we have already made will be carried forward to the market results and clean energy economy we seek.

Getting this money into the economy quickly, carefully, and transparently is a top priority for me. . . .

We have put in place a set of processes in the Department [of Energy] to get Recovery Act funds out the door quickly to good projects, with an unprecedented degree of transparency. This will make a significant down payment toward the nation's energy and environmental policy goals. With this Recovery Act spending, we are creating jobs and we are providing incentives for private capital to move off the sidelines and back into the energy markets.

Investing in New Energy Technology

With that, I would like to turn to a topic that is near and dear to my heart: how we can better nurture and harness science to solve our energy and climate change problems. I have spent most of my career in research labs—as a student, as a researcher, and as a faculty member. I took the challenge of being secretary of Energy in part for the chance to ensure that the Department of Energy [DOE] laboratories and our country's universities will generate ideas that will help us address our energy challenges. I also strongly believe that the key to our prosperity in the 21st century lies in our ability to nurture our intellectual capital in science and engineering. Our previous investments in science led to the birth of the semiconductor [technology used in modern computers], computer, and biotechnology industries that have added greatly to our economic prosperity. Now, we need similar breakthroughs on energy.

We're already taking steps in the right direction, but we need to do more.

First, we need to increase funding. As part of the president's plan to double federal investment in the basic sciences, the 2010 budget provides substantially increased support for the Office of Science, building on the $1.6 billion provided in the Recovery Act for the Department of Energy's basic sciences programs.

We also need to refocus our scarce research dollars. In April, a more detailed FY [fiscal year] 2010 budget will be transmitted to Congress. This budget will improve energy research, development, and deployment at DOE: by developing science and engineering talent; by focusing on transformational research; by pursuing broader, more effective collaborations; and by improving connections between DOE research and private sector energy companies.

Several years ago, I had the honor and privilege of working on the *Rising Above the Gathering Storm* report of the National Academy of Sciences. One of the report's key recommendations is to step up efforts to educate the next generation of scientists and engineers. The FY 2010 budget supports graduate fellowship programs that will train students in energy-related fields. I will also seek to build on DOE's existing research strengths by attracting and retaining the most talented scientists.

Energy Research Yields Results

The second area that I want to discuss is the need to support transformational technology research. What do I mean by transformational technology? I mean technology that is game-changing, as opposed to merely incremental. For example, in the 1920s and 1930s, when AT&T Bell Laboratories was focused on extending the life of vacuum tubes, another much smaller research program was started to investigate a completely new device based on a revolutionary new advance in the understanding of the microscopic world: quantum physics. The result of this transformational research was the transistor, which transformed communications, allowed the computer industry to blossom, and changed the world forever.

Government Investment Should Be Broad

While Washington [the U.S. capital] should flood the zone with research funding, it should refrain from trying to pick a winner. The great biofuel scam—in which government support for corn ethanol choked the market with a fuel that simply adds to other problems, such as deforestation and food price spikes—shows that straightforward subsidies can easily be perverted for political reasons. But a national renewable portfolio standard, which would mandate that a certain percentage of the nation's electricity supply must come from renewable sources, can force utilities to adopt alternatives on a wider scale, going with the technologies that are producing the best results. For that to happen, though, the government has to stop providing the fossil fuel industry with billions of dollars in subsidies, which boost the sector's built-in advantage even more.

Bryan Walsh,
"How to Win the War on Global Warming,"
Time, April 28, 2008.

DOE must strive to be the modern version of the old Bell Labs in energy research. Because the payoffs from research in transformational technologies are both higher risk and longer term, government investment is critical and appropriate.

Here is an example of current DOE transformational research. As this committee knows, we have funded three Bioenergy Research Centers—one at the Oak Ridge National Laboratory in Oak Ridge, Tennessee; one led by the University of Wisconsin in Madison, Wisconsin, in close collaboration with Michigan State University in East Lansing, Michigan; and one led by the Lawrence Berkeley National Laboratory. Each of these centers is targeting breakthroughs in biofuel technology development that will be needed to make abundant, affordable, low-carbon biofuels a reality. While these efforts are still relatively new, they are already yielding results, such as the bioengineering of yeasts that can produce gasoline-like fuels, and the development of improved ways to generate simple sugars from grasses and waste biomass.

Alternative Energies to Research

We need to do more transformational research at DOE to bring a range of clean energy technologies to the point where the private sector can pick them up, including:

1. Gasoline and diesel-like biofuels generated from lumber waste, crop wastes, solid waste, and non-food crops;

2. Automobile batteries with two to three times the energy density that can survive 15 years of deep discharges;

3. Photovoltaic solar power that is five times cheaper than today's technology;

4. Computer design tools for commercial and residential buildings that enable reductions in energy consumption of up to 80 percent with investments that will pay for themselves in less than 10 years; and

5. Large-scale energy storage systems so that variable renewable energy sources such as wind or solar power can become base load power generators.

This is not a definitive list or a hard set of technology goals, but it gives a sense of the types of technologies and benchmarks I think we should be aiming for. We will need transformational research to attain these types of goals. To make it happen, we will need to re-energize our national labs as centers of great science and innovation.

Innovation and Cooperation Within the Department of Energy

At the same time, we need to seek innovation wherever it can be found—the new Advanced Research Projects Agency-Energy (ARPA-E) will open up research funding to the best minds in the country, wherever they may he. ARPA-E will identify technologies with the potential to become the next generation of revolutionary energy systems and products, which will make a major impact on our twin problems of energy security and climate change. . . .

ARPA-E will accomplish its mission by funding high-risk, high-payoff R&D [research and development], performed by industry, academia, not-for-profits, national laboratories, and consortia. ARPA-E will bring the DARPA [Defense Advanced Research Projects Agency, responsible for military technological development within the U.S. Department of Defense]-style of transformational R&D management to focus on energy problems and opportunities. I pledge to you we will have this program up and running as soon as possible.

DOE also needs to foster better research collaboration, both internally and externally. My goal is nothing less than to build research networks within the department, across the government, throughout the nation, and around the globe. We'll better integrate national lab, university, and industry research. And we will seek partnerships with other nations. For example, increased international cooperation on carbon capture and storage technology could reduce both the cost and time of developing the range of pre- and post-combustion technologies needed to meet the climate challenge.

While we work on transformational technologies, DOE must also improve its efforts to demonstrate next-generation technologies and to help deploy demonstrated clean energy technologies at scale. The loan guarantee program will be critical to these efforts by helping to commercialize technologies, and the Recovery Act funding for weatherization and energy efficiency block grant programs will accelerate the deployment of energy efficient technologies.

The Government's Role in Developing Energy Alternatives

I am excited about the prospect of improving DOE's clean energy research, development, and deployment efforts. The nation needs better technologies to fully meet our climate and energy challenges, and DOE can be a major contributor to this effort.

We already have ample technology to make significant, near-term progress toward our energy and climate change goals. The most important of these is energy efficiency, which will allow us to reduce costs and conserve resources while still providing the same energy services. The potential there is huge, as is the potential to increase the use of existing technologies such as wind, solar, and nuclear. We will move forward on all of these fronts and more, as we invest in the transformational research to achieve breakthroughs that could revolutionize our nation's energy future.

*"The Obama energy plan . . . will likely
be used as a case study in college classes
generations from now as a lesson explaining how government interference
in the markets leads to the economic
downfall of a civilization."*

Government Programs Would
Be Ineffective at Developing
Alternative Energy

Ed Hiserodt

*Following his election in 2008, President Barack Obama set forth
an energy plan that detailed specific ways to decrease American
energy consumption and reduce reliance on foreign oil. Ed Hiserodt dissects this plan in the following viewpoint, pointing out
what he sees as the flaws of each of the president's suggested
courses of action. Hiserodt argues that the president's plan will
produce no net reduction in the country's energy needs nor advance energy alternatives. In his gravest prediction, the author
asserts that the plan's interference in the free market could result*

Ed Hiserodt, "Green Fairy Tales," *New American*, vol. 25, June 22, 2009, pp. 11–17.
Copyright © 2009 American Opinion Publishing Incorporated. Reproduced by permission.

in the end of American civilization as it exists today. Hiserodt is an aerospace engineer and regular contributor to the conservative magazine the New American.

As you read, consider the following questions:

1. What are some of the problems with the government's planned proliferation of plug-in hybrid electric vehicles, according to Hiserodt?

2. In Hiserodt's opinion, how many conventional power plants would be eliminated with the widespread use of solar power?

3. What danger does the introduction of wind power to an electric grid pose, as reported by the author?

The [Barack] Obama administration plans to turn conventional wisdom on its ear, advancing a plan wherein, instead of increasing energy supplies, the United States will attempt to decrease energy usage and replace our present reliable energy supply with solar- and wind-energy alternatives. The administration encapsulates its "New Energy for America" plan in six sentence-long bullet points, which we quote verbatim below:

- Provide short-term relief to American families facing pain at the pump

- Help create five million new jobs by strategically investing $150 billion over the next ten years to catalyze private efforts to build a clean energy future

- Within 10 years save more oil than we currently import from the Middle East and Venezuela combined

- Put 1 million plug-in hybrid cars—cars that can get up to 150 miles per gallon—on the road by 2015, cars that we will work to make sure are built here in America

- Ensure 10 percent of our electricity comes from renewable sources by 2012, and 25 percent by 2025

- Implement an economy-wide cap-and-trade program to reduce greenhouse gas emissions 80 percent by 2050

Let's now take a look at the plan in detail.

The Dangers of Increasing Miles-per-Gallon Mandates

To moderate the pain of paying high gas prices, the Obama administration plans to confiscate a "reasonable share" (you might guess who is to determine what is "reasonable") of record-breaking "windfall profits" of the oil companies and give it to American families as an "emergency energy rebate." Individuals would receive a $500 largesse, while couples would be blessed with $1,000. Note that this subsidy tends to increase demand, while stripping profits from the oil company not only harms innocent stockholders and pension funds (which pay for people's retirement), but reduces the capital to find and develop new sources of oil thus driving the price of fuel up—starting another round of subsidies, penalties, and higher prices.

In addition to the "pain" additional government interference in the energy market will cause, we'll experience new "pain at the showroom." The Obama administration proposed that Corporate Average Fuel Economy (CAFE) standards increase the fleet average requirement by 2016 to 35.5 miles per gallon from the present rate of 27.5 for cars and 24.0 for light trucks. The engineering to accomplish this feat comes with a healthy price tag or $1,300 per vehicle according to administration estimates, though engineering and fuel economy experts predict a rise of between $5,000 and $12,000. And the economic pain would be exacerbated by the physical pain and death caused by the lighter vehicles required to meet the CAFE requirements. Dr. Leonard Evans, author of *Traffic Safety*, concludes that "CAFE kills, and higher CAFE standards will kill even more."

Hybrid Vehicles Are Impractical for Most Americans

According to Obama, America needs to reduce oil consumption through switching to efficient vehicles. He would, he said, "put one million plug-in hybrid cars—cars that can get up to 150 miles per gallon—on the road by 2015, cars that we will work to make sure are built here in America." Is this feasible? And what effect will this have?

Let's look at car technology. The conventional hybrid car available today, such as the Toyota Prius, is not a plug-in hybrid electric vehicle (PHEV), as referred to by Obama. Today's hybrids typically have batteries, which are used for low-speed operation, and gasoline engines, which kick in at higher speeds and charge the batteries. The cars also have regenerative braking, meaning that in stop-and-go traffic the kinetic energy of the car is used to charge the battery during braking.

Toyota hopes to be the first competitor in the plug-in hybrid market in 2010 with a PHEV-7 car—a car that can travel seven miles on battery-only power. The GM [General Motors] Volt, also hoping to see the sales floor with a 2010 model, is a plug-in that would get 40 miles per charge. When battery power is exhausted, a gasoline engine drives a generator that provides electricity directly to the axle-mounted DC [direct current] motors. There will certainly be customers for this type of automobile—especially those with short commutes, a garage (no stringing electrical cords across the sidewalk or using half the battery power for heating the car in the morning), and a fairly healthy car budget. The price tag is expected to be about $42,000—but then the plan is to give buyers a $7,500 tax credit (not just a tax deduction), paid for primarily by those who can't afford a $42,000 or even a $31,500 compact car.

Not expected to be interested in cars like the Volt: soccer moms, interstate drivers (the 68 hp [horsepower] engine is considerably less powerful than a twin-cam Harley), anyone who may need to tow something someday, and others who just don't want to go to the extra effort of making sure their car is tucked into bed every night.

Let's put this program into perspective, shall we? As of 2006, there were over 240 million cars, pickups, minivans, and SUVs [sport-utility vehicles] registered in the United States. The one million PHEVs sought by Obama amount to 0.4 percent of the total passenger fleet. The decrease in petroleum-product usage we could expect if one out of every 240 vehicles used nothing but electricity would be minimal. Is this something the federal government should be concerned over, or is it feel-good pandering to the radical environmentalists and journalist *ignorati* [slang term referring to elite, uninformed individuals]?

Alternatives to Gasoline Are Limited

The overall goal of the Obama administration is to, within 10 years, save more oil than we currently import from the Middle East and Venezuela combined. But how much oil is that, and how much oil usage do we still need to cut after putting the PHEVs on the road?

The Middle East and Venezuela combined provide about 1.34 billion barrels of oil per year—some 37 percent of the 3.6 billion barrels in total imports. Of the total domestic and imported oil, 1.34 billion barrels is about 19 percent of total consumption. Where do we begin to increase supply or decrease demand to offset roughly one in five gallons of oil?

Let's start with those million PHEV cars, which, for simplicity's sake, we'll assume don't use any petroleum fuels.

For the same reason, we'll double those PHEVs to two million, so we can figure to have a one-percent oil-consumption reduction—only 18 percent to go.

Can we save more by using ethanol as a substitute for petroleum? Oops, we're already going down that road and are very near to an "ethanol bubble" in this correspondent's opinion. Yes, there are some happy farmers and some happy (and rich) blenders of ethanol into various gasohol concoctions. But there are also some very unhappy people—especially in the poorer countries—who have seen the price of staples like tortillas double in price. Burning our food as fuel has also caused serious increased costs in livestock production following higher feed prices. With 27 recent bankruptcies of ethanol producers, many investors in ethanol plants are whistling through the graveyard these days hoping to recoup their investments without anyone noticing they are bailing out. . . .

Of course, there are ways to increase the availability of U.S. crude (such as developing our offshore and Alaskan fields) and methods to provide ample crude-oil substitutes (such as converting coal into liquid fuel as was done by the Germans during WWII [World War II] and is still being done in South Africa). Using the high temperatures of pebble bed nuclear reactors, this could be done efficiently and with little pollution, but it will never happen under this administration as there is no intent to produce more energy—only an intent to use less.

Focusing Only on Solar and Wind Power

Advancing hand in hand with reducing oil consumption is the administration's plan to "ensure that 10 percent of our electricity comes from renewable sources by 2012 and 25 percent by 2025"—moving our country away from CO_2 [carbon dioxide]-emitting power sources to "clean, abundant power."

Since Obama said on December 20, 2007, that he is "not a nuclear power proponent," and there is no record that he has since reversed that position, one can assume America's new green energy will not be nuclear. And since he will only back coal as a power source if it involves the capture and storage of CO_2, and such "capturing" processes are strictly in experimental stages, we can bypass that option as well.

Inasmuch as Obama has barely given lip service to geothermal energy, when he says "renewables," he means solar energy and wind power. Let us take a practical look at these as energy sources for America.

Solar Power Cannot Replace Existing Power Plants

Since the deserts of the western United States have 280 clear days per year and solar energy is there for the taking—as compared to some 120 such days in the northeastern United States—it seems like a no-brainer to build a power line from the sun-rich desert to the energy-starved states of the Northeast. (Twenty-five percent of U.S. electrical energy—1,004 of 4,157 million megawatt-hours—is used in the industrial states of Illinois, Indiana, Pennsylvania, Ohio, Michigan, New Jersey, and New York.) Problem solved! Planet saved! Why then is solar only a tiny fraction of one percent of U.S. energy production—and losing ground?

Before America starts building a transmission network to transfer this energy (call it a Smart Grid since "smart" stuff is really *in* these days), we need to consider why private industry is *not* collecting all of this "free" power.

While there are up to 280 clear days in the desert, that also means there are about 85 days that aren't clear—in fact, they may be overcast and rainy. Even Death Valley has 18 days per year with measurable precipitation. Since electricity must be generated at the time it is used, what are we to do when the sun doesn't shine?

When the coffee pots and hair dryers are cranking up in the industrial Northeast, it is still dark in the desert. And it will be functionally "dark" until about 2 p.m. EST [Eastern

California's Disastrous Energy Policy

Governor Arnold Schwarzenegger and some prominent members of Congress from California, have touted California's energy and global warming policies as a successful model for the nation to follow. A paper published by CEI [Competitive Enterprise Institute] by Tom Tanton, a leading expert on California's energy policy, demonstrates the falsity of these claims in detail. California's economy is in free fall and high energy prices are one of the causes. It is true that per capita carbon dioxide emissions have remained flat in California for many years, but that result has been achieved by driving energy-intensive industries out of California. For example, only a small fraction of the vehicles sold in California every year are now produced in California. They are produced in states with lower energy prices and higher per capita carbon emissions.

Myron Ebell, testimony before the U.S. House of Representatives Committee on Energy and Commerce, Washington, DC, April 22, 2009.

Standard Time] when the incidence of the sun's ray allows the photovoltaics (or the mirrors in a thermal plant) to collect sufficient energy for electricity generation to commence. Perhaps the government could decree that the East Coast go on "Green Time," where citizens would be required to stay in bed till 2 p.m. (Teenagers would certainly be for it.)

If we are to supply even 10 percent of the aforementioned states' electrical energy in the eight-hour period when there is sufficient sunlight, then we would need a transmission capacity of about 35,000 megawatts. A 345-kilovolt line with 1,000-amp conductors can carry about 500 megawatts, meaning it would take some 70 transmission lines crossing mountains, rivers, and the property of several hundred thousand possibly unimpressed landowners. (And for two-thirds of each day, these hundreds of thousands of 15-story towers would be nonfunctioning.)

As a matter of fact, tapping into solar power wouldn't lead to the elimination of any conventional power plants, since the solar-generated electricity is not available on demand. Conventional power plants must always be on standby, powered up as "spinning reserves" available at a moment's notice, just in case clouds or one of the frequent desert dust storms knocks out solar production. These reserves would have to come from natural-gas turbine generators or from coal or nuclear power plants that are running but are putting out less-than-maximum electricity so that they can come up to speed quickly when the solar generation drops off.

But what about periods such as the Northeast's morning peak when *no* solar is available? Then we would need our full existing complement of coal and nuclear power plants to provide the required energy. Since these plants require hours, if not days, to come online, they would need to stay in a full operational mode at all times. . . .

The Wind Is Not Always Blowing

Logic would suggest that if wind power were a viable option to other forms of generation, the investor-owned power companies would be first in line to utilize this "fuel-free" source of energy. If they did not utilize it, competitors would gain an advantage and abscond with valuable commercial and industrial accounts. Obviously, there is no such rush for wind power, as utilities must deliver electricity, not rhetoric.

The employment of wind-power electrical generation requires a modification of the normal rules of mathematics. Take the following question:

You have a 5,000-megawatt network of coal, nuclear, and natural-gas power plants, to which you add one hundred 1.5-megawatt wind turbines. What is your new capacity?

You still have a 5,000-megawatt network. The 150 megawatts of wind power don't count—because they can't be depended upon when electric energy is called for by the network.

An NPR (National Public Radio) interview of grid manager Bob Benbow made clear that he is worried that when wind power makes up a significant portion of his grid, managing it will cause him major problems because of grid instability, as happened to colleagues in Texas on February 29, 2008. The limit of wind power and/or solar power that can be added to a network is reported to be in the area of 9 percent, after which there becomes a danger of losing control of the network. Benbow elaborated on his concern about the possibility of 20-percent wind power on his grid: "If the wind is not blowing, you just don't have that resource available." And even when the wind is blowing there are problems with wind turbines: "A lot of these plants are not manned—if we need to turn them off, we have to send a person out to actually do that."

Other concerns frustrate Benbow and his fellows: Wind blows hardest at night when electricity demand is lowest, and it can't be counted on for hot summer days when it's needed most: "You can put all that wind in, but I still need to have all this other generation that I need to have available—all my coal, nuclear, all the gas—for my peak load day." It's not easy being green. . . .

Energy Alternatives and Lost Jobs

Of course, if solar and wind power aren't viable, neither is the claim by Obama that his administration will "help create five million new jobs by strategically investing $150 billion over the next ten years to catalyze private efforts to build a clean energy future."

Again, we look to what's happening in Europe—as Obama did, after a fashion, in a speech in March [2009] given at the Southern California Edison Electric Vehicle Technical Center. "Around the world nations are racing to lead these industries of the future," he said. "Spain," the president reported, "generates almost 30 percent of its power by harnessing the wind, while we manage less than one percent."

A recent study by researchers at Spain's King Juan Carlos University [Universidad Rey Juan Carlos] looked closely at the idea that new green energy jobs will stimulate hiring across the economy:

> We find that for every renewable energy job that the State manages to finance, Spain's experience cited by President Obama as a model reveals with high confidence, by two different methods, that the U.S. should expect a loss of at least 2.2 jobs on average, or about 9 jobs lost for each 4 created, to which we have to add those jobs that non-subsidized investments with the same resources would have created. . . .

Why is the Obama administration overlooking the *real* European example? Because in the administration's worldview, the only important factor is controlling how much "greenhouse gas" is produced. This makes sense when you put the administration's energy puzzle together and look at the biggest piece—cap and trade.

Cap and Trade Is Rationing

The Obama administration plans to "implement an economy-wide cap-and-trade program to reduce greenhouse gas emissions 80 percent by 2050."

Cap and trade—just kind of rolls off your tongue. Having become such a common phrase, it's lost all sense of harshness and severity. There is another word that means the same thing, although for most Americans it has also lost its sense of authoritarian control: r-a-t-i-o-n-i-n-g. In this case we are not rationing to provide supplies for troops, as in WWII, but rationing industry's ability to produce goods and services that would improve the condition of humanity. All this in order to avert a hypothetical global warming crisis for future generations. . . .

At the beginning, the enforcement of the carbon-reduction scheme would be arranged through regulations on electric power companies, motor fuel companies, and other large users of carbon-based energy. But in time, the scheme would become not only a tax burden for consumers, but a bureaucratic one: When ABC Power Company is forced to decrease its carbon emissions, and the windmills can't take up the slack, then its customers would be squeezed. ABC Power would have to ration the amount of power each customer may use. If a customer exceeds his allowed usage, then the meter would be turned off, or a surcharge would apply based on the trading on carbon credits done by the utility. Similarly, gasoline will become in short supply, requiring rationing to keep the oil companies from exceeding their supply of carbon credits. To say this would create the bureaucracy of all bureaucracies is an understatement.

The Downfall of a Civilization

If it's enacted, the Obama energy plan, if it can be called that, will likely be used as a case study in college classes generations from now as a lesson explaining how government interference in the markets leads to the economic downfall of a civilization.

| "Data show that investing $100 billion in the green economy can create 2 million good jobs in the next two years."

The Government Should Subsidize the Creation of Green Jobs

Melissa Bradley-Burns

Some experts tout green jobs—jobs that involve the development, production, installation, and maintenance of environmentally friendly products and services—as a solution to the recession in the United States. After explaining how government subsidies could serve as a catalyst for a green economy, Melissa Bradley-Burns argues in the following viewpoint that the government subsidization of green jobs is essential to restoring the U.S. economy. To illustrate her point, she describes specific historical and contemporary cases in which government investment in private industry increased employment and helped develop companies that prosper today. While Bradley-Burns believes that government incentive can spur economic growth, she also encourages government oversight to measure the progress of individual businesses and penalize businesses that misuse federal funds. Bradley-

Melissa Bradley-Burns, "Why the Federal Government Should Subsidize Green Jobs and Keep Americans Out of Poverty," Green for All, February 23, 2009. www.greenforall.org. Reproduced by permission.

Burns is a senior strategist for Green for All, an organization dedicated to promoting the growth of a green economy in the United States.

As you read, consider the following questions:

1. What points does Bradley-Burns use as evidence of market demand and opportunity for the creation of green jobs?

2. What four comprehensive federal government programs does the author believe would increase green investment and the creation of green jobs?

3. According to the author, what guidelines would help ensure the growth and prosperity of a green economy?

The role of government is to instill confidence in the American public and support citizens in their belief that our social and financial well-being is real. With respect to our current crises, it is the job of government to restore confidence in and stability to our economy and our country. This role is also an opportunity: Strong government action now can help reinvigorate our economy, make our nation more environmentally friendly, and provide jobs to millions of poor workers.

The current credit and environmental crises cannot be solved by the private sector alone. First, the banking crisis has virtually dried up access to capital and thus constrains companies' ability to hire, invest, innovate, and jump-start the economy. Moreover, the wave of corruption within corporate America has caused mistrust of the private sector.

President Franklin D. Roosevelt once said, "The practices of unscrupulous money changers stand indicted in the court of public opinion, rejected by the hearts and minds of men and women. . . . The money changers have fled from their high seats in the temple of our civilization." Over 50 years later, this statement is still relevant. Therefore, the government must intervene to restore faith in the American dream and create and catalyze markets that can create jobs and save the environment.

John Maynard Keynes argued for government spending as a vehicle for recovery. By using fiscal policy, the government can provide a stimulus and multiplier effect. This multiplier effect, initiated in the public sector, can be scaled within the private sector. This is our opportunity for today.

Subsidies are not new. In fact, this country has a history of subsidies, or investments, that have yielded significant social and financial returns. For example, the New Deal prevented the economy from decaying further by increasing regulatory functions of the federal government in ways that helped stabilize previous trouble areas of the economy: the stock market, banking, and others. Moreover, the New Deal spent $3.3 billion with private companies to build over 30,000 projects. One of the results of Roosevelt's hard work over 12 years was an 8.5 percent compound annual growth of GDP—the highest growth rate in the history of any industrial country. Other successes included the consumer price index (CPI) increasing to over 100 from just over 90 in 1933. Exports increased almost fourfold from 1933 to 1940.

Another example of government subsidies is funds disbursed to "Small Business Investment Companies" (SBIC). Created by Congress in 1958, the SBIC was to bridge the gap between entrepreneurs' need for capital and traditional financing sources. It started as a multibillion-dollar, government-sponsored "fund of funds" that invested long-term capital in privately owned and managed investment firms (licensees); truly a public-private partnership. Since its inception, the fund has put money in over 370 private equity partnerships and supported diverse private partners providing roughly $9.4 billion in capital resources to small businesses nationwide. In 2007, SBIC financings totaled $2.7 billion, with

2,057 companies benefiting from SBIC financing. Companies that were successful because of SBIC include: America Online, Apple, Amgen, Costco, Intel, Orbital Sciences, Sun Microsystems, and WebMethods.

Today, critical legislation and key sector investments can provide a similar stimulus to the economy. For example, the Green Jobs Act of 2007 is supporting training programs to create a pipeline of workers to efficiency, biofuels, retrofits, and renewables.

America has lost over 3 million jobs in recent months, with 600,000 lost in January alone. Last year's fourth quarter unemployment rate was 6.6 percent, an increase of about 140 percent over the same period the year before.

Data show that investing $100 billion in the green economy can create 2 million good jobs in the next two years. Therefore, the creation of green jobs—providing living wages for infrastructural and environmental work in our nation's cities—is a great catalyst for rescuing the economy. But to create a green jobs economy, we're going to need government help.

Jobs are based on market demand. In the case of subsidies, government can jump-start demand that can be advanced and scaled by the private sector. Evidence of market demand and opportunities include:

- Between now and 2030, 75 percent of the buildings in the United States will either be new or substantially rehabilitated.

- In 2006, the "Green-tech" sector was the third largest represented globally and $3.6 billion was poured into companies last year.

- In 2006, renewable energy and energy efficiency technologies generated 8.5 million new jobs, nearly $970 billion in revenue, and more than $100 billion in industry profits.

- If 50 percent of the 128 million housing units nation-wide are retrofitted at the modest rate of $10,000 per unit, it would create a retrofit market worth over $600 billion in revenues.

- The United States' solar energy market has seen fantastic growth over the last five years, and global solar market capitalization is well over $500 billion.

- In 2006, the renewable energy and energy efficiency industries created 8.5 million jobs. With continued investment by the government, the jobs could top 40 million by 2030.

Now is a key moment to capitalize on this growing market. One element of the stimulus bill is to double clean energy production in three years, weatherize 2 million homes, and create a half million jobs in the clean energy sector. This is a pivotal opportunity to invest in green jobs and clean energy infrastructure, which will make our economy stronger and more stable.

Public officials have the opportunity and obligation to use tools at their disposal to catalyze certain industry sectors and hold employers accountable for creating good jobs. Subsidies are one of their tools. There are at least four comprehensive programs the federal government can initiate to spur green energy investment and put money in the hands of workers who need it most:

1. Establish an energy-efficient retrofits program for public and private buildings, which can jump-start the construction industry.

2. Require all workers on projects or contracts supported by federal funds be paid a wage that will keep them out of poverty. This will stimulate local economies and ultimately increase local tax revenue.

3. Incentivize the development of a green manufacturing industry. Historically, manufacturing has always provided a key opportunity for growth in the United States.

4. Increase government contracting for goods and services as a means to jump-start local economies. As municipal budgets spiral downward, the federal government can encourage local governments to maintain policies that support economic development, not outsourcing. For example, the federal government could require responsible contractor policies when federal funds pay for all or part of locally procured goods and services.

It is important to note that not all subsidies are new and subsidies are not the only source of funding or investment. In most cases, government subsidies are best when they successfully leverage additional investment. Examples include:

- Clipper Windpower in Cedar Rapids, Iowa, where subsidies of just over $3 million supported $50 million of total investment.

- Vestas Americas in Brighton, Colorado, received $8.5 million in subsidies toward a total investment of $240 million and created a minimum of 1,300 jobs.

- SolarWorld in Hillsboro, Oregon, received $41 million for a total investment of $440 million and created at minimum 1,000 jobs.

It is important to note that subsidies are not intended to be a blank check for the public or private sector. Rather, subsidies are about making good investments that yield a return. Good investments will be measured through return on investment, and it is important for the government to establish benchmarks and guidelines to be sure it gets a good deal. Some of these stipulations should include:

- Clear milestones with audit function and repercussions for failed opportunities.

- Clear "return on investment" benchmarks to be mutually and explicitly agreed upon.

- Use of "clawbacks" (money that can be recovered according to agreed upon terms) that provide accountability and enforcement, allowing government to recapture funds when contractors fail to meet standards.

- Inclusion of a domestic sourcing requirement attached to subsidies so that American taxpayers can reap the greatest benefit.

Subsidies should be viewed as a tool for leverage and a means to catalyze private sector growth.

In the case of our current economic and environmental crises, the focus on improving efficiency and lowering energy costs of existing infrastructure while creating jobs is a smart investment. It is an opportunity to promote high-quality, family-supporting jobs in the United States, support low-income communities in accessing high-quality jobs, and create an inclusive economy.

The time is now for green jobs to help reverse the economic and climate crises in this country. However, like all major market transformations, this movement will require huge amounts of social, financial, and human capital.

> *"Consumers currently do not choose to voluntarily hand over enough money for the products and services created by green jobs otherwise they wouldn't need such a lavish government subsidy in the first place."*

The Government Should Not Subsidize the Creation of Green Jobs

Institute for Energy Research

While proponents of green jobs—jobs selling environmentally friendly goods and services—contend that government investment in a green economy will jump-start the American economy, critics believe the cost to create these jobs is too high. For example, the Institute for Energy Research (IER) asserts, in the viewpoint that follows, that green jobs are too expensive for the government to subsidize, with cost estimates ranging from $30,000 to $100,000 per job. The institute also maintains that it is unfair to use taxpayer dollars—earned in jobs that were not created using government subsidies—to fund an industry that cannot sustain itself, much less grow, based on market demand.

The Institute for Energy Research is a nonprofit energy research institute that advocates a free market approach to global energy policy.

As you read, consider the following questions:

1. What is great about a market economy, according to the IER?

2. What are two companies cited by the IER that have profited without government investment?

3. What long-term impact does the IER believe the economic inefficiency of green jobs has on the country?

The term "green job" has been invented to describe the type of workforce needed to build a new government-funded national "alternative" energy infrastructure. Proponents of "green jobs" say that by spending taxpayer money on energy sources like wind and solar [power], the government can create millions of new jobs in the process. But according to the biggest proponents, such a program would cost taxpayers somewhere between $30,000 and $ 100,000 per new job.

The Benefits of a Market Economy

During the campaign, President-elect [Barack] Obama said he would like to dedicate $15 billion in taxpayer funds to create "green jobs." Spending billions to create jobs sounds appealing, but Obama and other proponents of such a program have thus far failed to mention the downsides this will have on the productivity of the overall economy.

One of the great things about a market economy is that politicians and government planners don't have to do anything for economic activity to take place. Bureaucrats don't need to invent nongovernment related jobs and subsidize them with taxpayer funds. They don't need to determine in which regions the jobs should be created and which skills are best suited for them. In a market economy, employees and employers make these determinations together. Entrepreneurs start new businesses and try to hire the best people for the jobs these businesses create. Nobody needs to check in with a government bureaucrat and it doesn't cost the taxpayer a dime. While not perfect, the entire process is remarkably efficient. Jobs are created to provide the goods and services that people want and need when they want and need them. And when consumers change their preferences, the economy adapts accordingly.

Successful Companies Don't Need Government Subsidies

Take Google, for example. Google was incorporated in September of 1998. By 2008, Google employed 20,000 people. It didn't cost the American people anything to create these jobs. But the American people, and the rest of the world, have benefited greatly from Google's excellent search engine and other innovative products like Google Maps, Google Earth, and Gmail.

Google shows us how jobs are created in a market economy. Without imposing on the American taxpayer, they made a superior product for consumers and 20,000 jobs have been created. As a result, humanity reaps the benefit of being able to use Google's superior products. And as an added bonus to the government, Google pays millions in taxes each year.

Consider ExxonMobil as another example. Even in these challenging economic times, ExxonMobil earned billions in profits, employs 80,800 employees, and pays billions of dollars in taxes and fees to the government every year. ExxonMobil makes money because people are willing to buy, without being forced by the government, ExxonMobil's gasoline and other products. When ExxonMobil hires a new employee, it doesn't receive money from the federal government to help create that new job, because ExxonMobil sells a product people will voluntarily buy.

So if Google and ExxonMobil can create jobs without federal subsidies and payments, why do so-called "green jobs" need to cost the American taxpayer so much? President-elect Obama says his 5 million new green jobs will cost $30,000 taxpayer dollars per job. And Obama's plan is far more optimistic than those of even his closest allies.

The Expense of Creating Green Jobs

The [liberal public policy organization] Center for American Progress (whose CEO [chief executive officer] heads Obama's transition team) calculates that it would take government spending of $100 billion to create 2 million jobs. By their calculations, it costs the taxpayer $50,000 to create a single "green job." The Apollo Alliance [a coalition of individuals seeking to expand and develop a green economy in the United States] (whose founder served on Obama's campaign staff) released a study, which calculates that it would take $500 billion in taxpayer dollars to create 5 million jobs. That works out to a taxpayer "investment" of $100,000 per green job.

These green jobs are awfully expensive. And even the Apollo Alliance admits [its] numbers have little basis in reality. According to the *Wall Street Journal*, "Kate Gordon, codirector of the Apollo Alliance, says the numbers are less important than the message. 'Honestly,' she says, 'it's just to inspire people.'"

Inspiration, it seems, is in the eye of the beholder, for it is hardly inspiring to consider that even with the president-elect's most optimistic assumptions, $30,000 in government subsidies are necessary to create every new government-inspired green job. And if such a plan is actually implemented, it might indeed create some new jobs, but it is also going to destroy a lot of existing jobs through the increased tax burden

Dangers of the Green-Industrial Complex

For [President Barack] Obama, it is the public impact of terms like "green jobs" and "green economy," and the ability of such new terms to force corporations to compete in a new way, that is really key. His embrace of the Green-Industrial Complex is not about affecting real change, far less about restructuring the economy in a way that might make it more productive. Rather, it is about instituting a new political outlook, one in which government intervention on the side of science-exploiting, globally-conscious corporations becomes the solution to contemporary problems. It is an outlook that both evades responsibility for overhauling the economy in a meaningful way and demotes individual initiative in favor of this burgeoning business/science/government alliance.

Indeed, green activists now talk openly about the recession being a "good thing." Not only will it lead to less "destructive" human activity because people will be so financially restricted they won't be able to consume and pollute in a wanton fashion, it will also elevate the policies of the Green-Industrial Complex to the center stage of public debate.

Brendan O'Neill, "Green-Industrial Complex,"
American Conservative, *August 1, 2009.*

necessary to carry out his plan. The $30,000 to $100,000 per job has to come from somewhere and that somewhere is people with real jobs today—working at Google or Exxon-Mobil for example—that pay taxes on the income they earn from their real job. These people didn't ask the government for a dime, nor were their jobs created by the government and yet they will be paying the Obama green jobs tax.

Green Jobs Fail the Market Test

Finally, the fact that Obama's green jobs require such lavish government subsidies is proof that they simply fail the market test. That is to say, consumers currently do not choose to voluntarily hand over enough money for the products and services created by green jobs otherwise they wouldn't need such a lavish government subsidy in the first place. This economic inefficiency will only make the country poorer in the long run. After all, you don't make consumers better off by forcing them to buy products and services that they wouldn't have purchased voluntarily in the first place.

> "The Obama administration has all the grounds it needs to declare an energy emergency and devote the country's vast talents and resources to responding."

It Is Unclear Whether President Obama's Energy Policies Go Far Enough to Save the Planet

Carl Etnier

Throughout his presidential campaign in 2008, Barack Obama made many promises to increase the use of alternative energy in the United States and move the country toward energy independence. Upon closer examination of his policy proposals, Carl Etnier worries that the president's energy policy will not be drastic enough to facilitate significant change. In the viewpoint that follows, Etnier argues that while Obama has made some important shifts away from what Etnier sees as poor policy suggestions— such as a gas tax holiday—the author worries that on other issues, such as transportation and nuclear energy, Obama's energy policies do not differ substantially from the previous administra-

tion's legislation. Still, the author remains hopeful that the nationwide awareness and support for energy alternatives will encourage President Obama to make the necessary changes to current energy policy and halt global warming. Etnier is the director of the Montpelier, Vermont, Peak Oil Awareness, an organization dedicated to educating the public about the decline of international oil reserves.

As you read, consider the following questions:

1. What parts of the Obama energy policy does the author find confusing?

2. In the author's view, how does Obama's energy plan serve as a continuation of previous policies regarding transportation?

3. While the author commends the president for addressing climate change, the creation of green jobs, and reducing dependence on foreign oil, what issue does he chide the president for not addressing?

President-elect Barack Obama's speech in Chicago's Grant Park last Tuesday night [November 4, 2008] was a celebration of his campaign victory. He didn't dwell on policy, nor should he have.

I was encouraged, however, that he included climate change and renewable energy among the few priorities he did highlight. With significant Democratic gains in Congress, Obama will have an opportunity to sign more significant energy-related legislation than we've seen since Jimmy Carter's presidency.

I wonder though whether it will be enough to prevent an energy-driven depression following the present economic turmoil.

The Urgent Need for Environmental Policy

Eight years ago, George W. Bush campaigned for the presidency on a promise to regulate carbon dioxide as a pollutant. When he was elected, he dismissed the promise almost immediately.

Obama will find it harder to renege on his commitment on climate change and energy policy. He doesn't have the ties to the oil industry that Bush and his administration brought with them to the White House, and the political landscape has changed.

Part of the change comes from new urgency. Rajendra Pachauri, the scientist and economist who heads the Nobel Prize-winning Intergovernmental Panel on Climate Change, told the *New York Times* last year, "If there's no action before 2012, that's too late. What we do in the next two to three years will determine our future. This is the defining moment."

Now, too, more Americans are clamoring for action on climate change. Step It Up [formed in October 2006 to advance a national climate change agenda] pressured presidential candidates to adopt pledges to achieve sweeping reductions in greenhouse gas emissions by 2050. Step It Up's successor organization, 350.org, is keeping up the pressure. Will Bates, one of the original Step It Up organizers, recently showed me how to use 350.org's Web page for e-mailing Barack Obama, urging him to attend the December negotiations in Poland to replace the Kyoto Protocol with a stronger agreement.

The constituency for a radically different energy policy is broad. The National Wildlife Federation [NWF] is traditionally the most conservative of environmental organizations. Don Hooper, the organization's New England regional coordinator, said NWF recently asked [its] members with hunting or fishing licenses about energy policy. An astounding 80 percent responded that they wanted the United States to draw 100 percent of its energy from renewable sources within 10 years.

Obama's Split from Previous Policy

Obama has responded to grassroots pressures for a better energy policy. Just a year ago, he didn't know whether to push for 50 percent or 80 percent reduction in greenhouse gas emissions by 2050, and he didn't seem to attach much importance to the difference. Contrast that with Senator Bernard Sanders, I-Vt. [Independent from Vermont], who took up former Sen. James Jeffords's mantle on energy issues. On his first day in the Senate, Sanders introduced a bill designed to achieve an 80 percent reduction in greenhouse gases by 2050. Obama had adopted the Jeffords/Sanders goal by early in the primary season.

Obama distinguished himself during the recent run-up in gasoline prices, refusing to pander to voters with a gas tax holiday proposal, as Sens. John McCain and Hillary Clinton did. However, after initially resisting, he succumbed to calls from Vermont Rep. Peter Welch and others to start draining the Strategic Petroleum Reserve, which was created to respond to interruptions in supply, not merely high prices. The *New York Times* pointed to Obama's sudden reversals on this issue and offshore drilling as evidence that it's impossible to hold a "grown-up conversation" about energy in this country.

Obama's campaign produced an eight-page energy policy including cap-and-trade auctions of carbon emission permits, which could raise large sums to fund other parts of his energy policy, like weatherizing a million low-income homes a year, workforce training for renewable energy and efficiency jobs, and tax credits for plug-in hybrids and other advanced vehicles.

Confusion Within the Obama Energy Plan

Some parts of the Obama energy plan are confusing. He embraced new nuclear power plants in his stump speech. Yet his plan says that issues like safe storage of nuclear waste must be addressed before any new plants are considered. No high-level nuclear waste generated in the last 65 years has yet been placed in safe, long-term storage. And Obama opposes the one plan the federal government has for long-term storage, dumping the waste in the Yucca Mountain facility in Nevada (a swing state where Obama campaigned heavily).

If safe storage of nuclear waste must merely be addressed before new nuclear plants are built, I suppose the Nuclear Regulatory Commission could hold a single hearing on the subject and then start approving new reactors. If Obama means that a facility capable of safely storing the country's high-level waste for 10,000 years or more must actually be built, then we're unlikely to ever see another nuclear power plant.

On ethanol, Obama seems to be shifting. Iowa corn farmers are an important constituency, and Obama endorsed sharp increases in ethanol production during the primary season.

Recently, a discussion participant at TheOilDrum.com [a discussion board about oil and energy issues] reports that an Obama adviser told him that "Obama gets it that ethanol is sort of a joke . . . So ethanol probably won't go any further. If you noticed in his most recent speeches he stopped saying 'ethanol' and started saying 'next generation biofuels.'"

Sure enough, the eight-page Obama energy plan does say "next generation biofuels" and omits corn ethanol.

Conservative Transportation Goals

On transportation, the Obama energy plan is no great shakes. It advocates further subsidies for poorly managed U.S. automakers and a large investment in plug-in hybrid cars. While there's a place for plug-in hybrids, they're a continuation of the car-centric culture that exacerbates U.S. dependence on foreign oil. I'd put rebuilding the passenger rail system as a much higher priority; it's not mentioned.

Maybe we'll see a resurgence of passenger rail with "Joe the Amtrak Rider" Biden as vice president. Biden is famous

Barriers to Improved Energy Policy

In the United States, at least two significant organizational barriers stand in the way of the implementation of a sensible energy policy. First, the U.S. government is not currently structured in a way that would allow it to forcefully confront the nation's current energy challenges. Second, government employees often are not trained in the methods needed to implement thoughtful energy strategies. . . .

No single department is responsible for ensuring that the country is making wise decisions regarding climate change or, more broadly, energy management. While there is a Department of Energy, civilian energy is a very small part of that department's activities. No single unit is in charge of scanning the environment and collecting information on climate change, analyzing that information, and transforming it into effective policy. The United States, like other nations, developed structures for historic and institutional reasons that have not been adapted to meet current threats. Working with Congress, the new administration needs to set up structures that are better suited to the development and implementation of wise energy decisions.

Max H. Bazerman,
"U.S. Energy Policy: Overcoming Barriers to Action,"
Environment, September 2009.

for daily commuting from Delaware to D.C. by train. Al Papp, vice president for the National Association of Railroad Passengers, says he is hopeful of Biden's support for their plan to greatly expand passenger rail.

Obama's energy plan addresses climate change and the twin economic issues of creating green jobs and staunching the outflow of money to pay for oil imports. It does not address peak oil or even implicitly address resource limits that could shape our goals.

Take, for example, the support of NWF's licensed hunters and fishermen for 100 percent renewable energy within 10 years. If that is a doable goal, one way to imagine achieving it is to ramp up production of biodiesel and ethanol and plug-in hybrids so the NWF members can drive 20 or 200 miles to their favorite hunting and fishing spots. I would suggest another alternative: They could sell their cars and hunt and fish within walking or bicycling distance, or use public transit.

Even without peak oil to contend with, the vision of walkable hunts is more technically achievable than a complete conversion of all vehicles to renewable energy in 10 years. Add in potentially steep declines in the availability of oil and other fossil fuels, and our ability to recreate a renewable energy alternative universe crimps dramatically.

The Support for Energy Solutions Is Growing

It takes energy to manufacture new cars and new biofuel facilities. With a massive commitment now, by an inspiring leader, I believe the United States could rapidly change its manufacturing. Franklin [D.] Roosevelt quashed manufacture of private cars during World War II to free up factories to construct planes, tanks and ships. The climate is near a tipping point, and oil depletion stares us in the face. The Obama administration has all the grounds it needs to declare an energy emergency and devote the country's vast talents and resources to responding.

Popular awareness of peak oil and of the importance of re-localization for survival arose with George W. Bush in the White House, pointed out Bart Anderson, editor of Energy

Bulletin.net, a news aggregator for peak oil and sustainability issues. Anderson was a guest on my radio show the day after the election, and he suggested that leaders in the new movement wrote off national action, because they saw no likelihood of meaningful response from the administration. With a new administration, and a Congress more concerned about energy issues, he says that thoughts are turning to national action.

If Congress and Obama decide to invest heavily in rail, weatherization, renewables, local food production and other aspects of resilient communities, we'll be able to make a transition far more quickly. There's a danger, however, that new infusions of money will not go to investments that are most useful at a future time, when we have half or a 10th of the oil we use now. Dinosaur industries may be poorly managed, but they can afford lobbyists. (Immediately after the election, the auto industry demanded another $25 billion from the feds.)

Local planning, local energy, [and] local food continue to be crucial. Just now, I have some amount of hope that competence and attention from the federal government can boost those efforts enough to make a huge difference in how prepared we are a decade from now.

> "The [Waxman-Markey energy] bill's
> 1,500 pages of economic central plan-
> ning are bound to result in rationed
> energy, loss of productive jobs, and
> higher costs and taxes."

President Obama's Energy Policies Will Be Costly for the American Public

William P. Hoar

Critics of President Barack Obama's energy policy assert that his plan will increase the cost of energy production, thus creating an increased burden on American consumers and taxpayers. In the viewpoint that follows, William P. Hoar elucidates this view and argues that Obama's energy plan will result not only in increased taxes and energy costs, but also in unemployment and energy rationing. Hoar accuses the president and his administration of downplaying the actual costs of a cap-and-trade policy to limit carbon dioxide emissions. Further, he maintains that the recent Waxman-Markey energy bill provides evidence of the failure of Obama's energy plans because numerous special interest

William P. Hoar, "Taxing Energy in the Name of Climate Change," *New American*, vol. 25, August 3, 2009, pp. 42–43. Copyright © 2009 American Opinion Publishing Incorporated. Reproduced by permission.

projects were attached to attract the votes of congressmen. Hoar is a writer for the conservative public policy organization the John Birch Society.

As you read, consider the following questions:

1. What are some of the additional costs of Obama's energy plans, as reported by the author?

2. According to analysis by the Heritage Foundation, as cited by Hoar, by how much would the Waxman-Markey energy bill increase taxes for a family of four by 2035?

3. Based on the author's argument, how would the president's energy plan impact the housing market?

One would like to believe that Barack Obama would tell the truth about the costs and other impacts of the energy-rationing plan he favors. And he actually did, at a past date, make a somewhat honest assessment of what would happen were a "cap-and-trade" system to be instituted.

He is not being candid now [in the summer of 2009], of course, when it counts. Still, Obama did acknowledge to the *San Francisco Chronicle* in a January 2008 interview: "Under my plan of a cap-and-trade system, electricity rates would necessarily skyrocket ... because I'm capping greenhouse gases, coal power plants, natural gas, you name it.... Whatever the plants were, whatever the industry was, they would have to retrofit their operations. That will cost money, and they will pass that [cost] on to consumers."

The Regressive Environmental Tax

Those additional costs would run to well more than the price of a stamp, as the president and his minions now claim—unless there are some shocking jumps in postage headed our way. The paltry cost projections squeezed out of the Environ-

Cartoon courtesy of www.thechillingeffect.org. Cartoon by Robert Lang.

mental Protection Agency [EPA] and Congressional Budget Office (CBO) largely ignore that this is a massive energy tax that will drive up costs of electricity and gasoline, for example, and result in the shipping of American jobs overseas to escape the regulatory burden to be placed on industry here. (Worse, the legislation also threatens to start a trade war unless foreign nations adopt similar carbon limits. Communist

China, one of the world's worst polluters, is assuredly not going to commit economic suicide in such a fashion.)

Let's look at some of those additional costs planned for us. Numerous studies refute the administration's low-balling. An analysis made by the Heritage Foundation [a conservative public policy organization], for instance, of the Waxman-Markey bill [a climate and energy bill also known as the American Clean Energy and Security Act] reported out of House Committee on Energy and Commerce took a more complete view than did those who are pushing the tax-and-regulation scheme.

Heritage's points can be summarized as follows: Unemployment would increase by nearly 2 million in 2012, the first year of the program, and would reach nearly 2.5 million in 2035, the last year of the analysis. The total loss in gross national product by 2035 would be $9.4 trillion. Refuting the president's claims, the analysis concludes that the national debt would blow up as the economy slowed, weighing down a family of four with $114,915 of additional national debt. Families would suffer, the analysis shows, since the legislation would slap the equivalent of a $4,609 tax on a family of four by 2035.

Even some prominent supporters are not buying the administration's line. Billionaire Warren Buffett, an Obama enthusiast, told CNBC that the bill was a "huge tax" and "fairly regressive" that will harm "an awful lot of people." Indeed.

Selling the Energy Policy to the Public

You may have noticed that this legislation was not pushed as a "global warming" bill. Other than the fact that there hasn't been any measurable global warming for more than a decade, this is because the Democrats' pollsters have found this to be a losing issue. A leaked memo from the public relations [PR] firm of Greenberg Quinlan Rosner Research advised that global warming should not be used as the "primary frame." Said the PR outfit, referring to the issue of global warming and their focus groups: "Almost no one in our groups expressed such concern; for most voters, global warming is not significant enough on its own to drive support for major energy reform." The PR folks also urged that the term "green" should be dropped: "'Green' is meaningless or confusing—the term 'clean' resonates with voters." You will note that the president, as quoted above, is following his marching orders.

You will also note that the administration does not come clean by admitting that this measure is really about taxing, rationing, eliminating consumer choices, and regulating. Remember the housing problems that helped throw the nation into a recession? This measure would make it more difficult to buy and build homes (costs will rise with a mandated increase in building codes) and to sell (a new energy assessment rating is required that will penalize you for owning an older home). You probably haven't heard the White House boast that the hydrocarbon tax bill is designed to make the entire country follow the rules of bankrupt California in terms of "energy efficiency."

High Costs for Limited Benefits

The bill's 1,500 pages of economic central planning are bound to result in rationed energy, loss of productive jobs, and higher costs and taxes—with all hydrocarbon use to be penalized because big-government eco-worshippers are willing to hamstring the economy based on computer extrapolations of what the weather might be in 50 or 100 years. (These same computer models cannot even replicate past temperature changes, let alone predict future ones.) And what would we get after a national energy tax is imposed to produce centrally planned austerity?

Well, the EPA says that even if carbon dioxide emissions were to be reduced by 60 percent by 2050 (extremely unlikely), the temperature of the planet would drop by an insignificant 0.1–0.2 degrees C[elsius] by the year 2095.

A Bill Written for Special Interests

The president laughably extolled the bill for being "carefully written." In fact, the 1,200-page bill was rushed to the floor with little or no time for congressmen to read, with another 300 or so pages added literally at 3 A.M. on the day of the vote, with all manner of goodies larded on to placate special interests. Even the sympathetic *New York Times* conceded it had grown "fat with compromises, carve-out concessions and out-and-out gifts intended to win the votes of wavering lawmakers and the support of powerful industries." If this measure were so marvelous, you wouldn't have to bribe legislators to vote for it.

To cite just a couple of examples, in exchange for his vote, Representative Alan Grayson (D-Fla.) got $50 million for a hurricane research center in Orlando, while Rep. Marcy Kaptur (D-Ohio) secured, as reported by the *Washington Times*, "a new federal power authority, similar to Washington state's Bonneville Power Administration, stocked with up to $3.5 billion in taxpayer money." In short, as the *Financial Times* put it, the new tax measure "creates a vastly complicated apparatus, a playground for special interests and rent-seekers, a minefield of unintended consequences."

Passing the Cost on to Consumers

The CBO was right—though not about the current estimate of costs touted by House Democrats. However, when Peter Orszag was the CBO head (he's now the head of the White House's Office of Management and Budget), he admitted that "price increases would be essential to the success of a cap-and-trade program." And Obama was correct—before he became president—when he acknowledged that "under my plan of a cap-and-trade system, electricity rates would necessarily skyrocket." He told the *San Francisco Chronicle* that, under his plan, "If somebody wants to build a coal-fired plant, they can. It's just that it will bankrupt them, because they are going to be charged a huge sum for all that greenhouse gas that's being emitted."

Now we are supposed to believe that the planet is going to be saved for the price of a postage stamp. In the bovine world, that would be termed bull emission.

Periodical Bibliography

The following articles have been selected to supplement the diverse views presented in this chapter.

Lester R. Brown	"Time for Plan B," *USA Today*, March 2007.
Lawrence P. Farrell Jr.	"Alternative Energy Needed for More than Just Cost Savings," *National Defense*, December 2008.
Joshua Green	"The Elusive Green Economy," *Atlantic*, July/August 2009.
Joe Klein	"What a New Energy Economy Might Look Like," *Time*, November 13, 2008.
Steve LeVine	"Can the Military Find the Answer to Alternative Energy?" *BusinessWeek*, August 3, 2009.
Robert J. Samuelson	"The Bias Against Oil and Gas," *Newsweek*, May 18, 2009.
Jesse Scanlon	"America's Green Policy Vacuum," *BusinessWeek Online*, February 11, 2008. www.businessweek.com.
Max Schulz	"How Much Will Obama's Green Jobs Cost?" *Human Events*, May 18, 2009.
Kimberley Strassel	"Alternative Fuel Folly," *Wall Street Journal*, April 17, 2009.
Liz Wolgemuth	"The Truth About All Those Green Jobs," *U.S. News & World Report*, March 25, 2009.

For Further Discussion

Chapter 1

1. Reread the viewpoints by David Strahan and Michael Lynch and then conduct some outside research on peak oil claims. Which side of this debate do you favor? Using assertions and empirical evidence from the viewpoints and the other research you consulted, explain whether you believe the reality of peak oil or the myth of peak oil should influence America's adoption of alternatives to fossil fuels.

2. George Allen insists that America can wisely shepherd its own energy resources to end reliance on foreign oil. Robert Bryce holds a contrary view, arguing that modern America has never produced enough energy domestically to meet its demands and, therefore, should accept that it is part of a global system of energy supply and demand. Do you think it is possible for America to achieve energy independence? What do you think are some of the pros and cons of such independence? Use arguments from the viewpoints and expand upon them to make your own claims.

Chapter 2

1. Both the first and second pairs of viewpoints in Chapter 2 examine whether the environmental benefits of certain alternative energies, clean coal and biofuels respectively, outweigh the potential environmental destruction that energy production from these sources would cause. Kari Lydersen argues that mining coal is so damaging to the environment that no clean coal technology can mitigate the disastrous effects of this process. Helena Paul makes

the case that the cultivation of plants for biofuels will have similarly catastrophic impacts on lands used by marginalized populations. On the other hand, Gregory H. Boyce maintains that the use of clean coal will produce near-zero emissions and provide a substantial energy source for the country, and Paul Bardos and his colleagues contend that biofuels can be planted on unused lands and actually restore the economy of people living there. Reread all four viewpoints and consider whether widespread environmental benefits warrant the destruction of limited environments. Do you think that in some cases it is acceptable to destroy land in one area if it benefits the whole of humanity? Explain your answer using quotes from the viewpoints for support.

2. What is the chief asset of biodiesel according to *Fuel Oil News*? Politicians and other experts have proposed renewable energy sources such as solar, wind, and geothermal power as potential alternatives to coal, fossil fuels, and natural gas. Both proponents of renewable resources, such as Chris Flavin and Janet Sawin, and opponents of these technologies, such as William Tucker, present numerous statistics to support their claims. Examine the statistics and arguments of these authors. Which viewpoint do you find more compelling? Do you think that renewable energy sources would ever be capable of replacing traditional energy sources? Cite specific statistics from the viewpoints when constructing your argument.

Chapter 3

1. What kind of argumentative strategy does Donnie Johnston use to claim that ethanol fuel should be abandoned? How does Tom Daschle's rhetorical practice differ from Johnston's strategy. Explain which viewpoint you

find more convincing and state whether the type of argument used in that viewpoint had any influence on your decision.

2. What is the chief asset of biodiesel, according to *Fuel Oil News*? What are the main drawbacks to biodiesel production in Max Schulz's view? Explain which of these concerns is most important to you and which should guide the country's policy regarding the expansion or restriction of biodiesel manufacturing.

Chapter 4

1. Much of the debate over the use of energy alternatives revolves around the question of who should be responsible for the majority of the research and development. Should the government take charge of gathering the teams and footing the bill, or should private industry drive the switch from old energy resources to new ones? The authors of the first two viewpoints in Chapter 4 take opposing views on the issue. The U.S. Secretary of Energy Steven Chu makes the case for the necessity of government involvement in the expansion of alternative energies. Ed Hiserodt critiques the participation of the government as unrealistic and ineffective at facilitating change. Do you agree with Chu or Hiserodt? Will government intervention improve and spread alternative energies, or will it only stifle innovation and increase cost? Conduct additional research into the free market approach versus government involvement to support your view.

2. In the aftermath of soaring energy prices and the economic collapse that occurred at the end of George W. Bush's presidency, the creation of jobs has become an important concern of many American citizens. President Barack Obama has made job creation through the expansion of green industry a key part of his energy policy. Others criticize this approach, citing high cost as an in-

hibitor to employment growth. Melissa Bradley-Burns explains her support for Obama's green economy, while the Institute for Energy Research highlights the prohibitive cost. Examine both the numbers and the humanitarian arguments presented in both viewpoints. Do you believe it is the government's responsibility to create jobs when the economy falters? If the government is going to subsidize the creation of jobs, should those jobs be environmentally friendly? Does the cost of creating these green jobs impact your decision? Do you think the benefits of creating green jobs would outweigh the costs? Use quotations from the viewpoints to support your argument.

3. Many critics, both liberal and conservative, have questioned the value of President Obama's energy policy. Go online and find an outline of Obama's energy proposal. After reading his suggestions, reread the final two viewpoints of Chapter 4. Do you think that one viewpoint has more merit than the other, or do you think that the authors of both viewpoints misread the proposal? Do you have a different understanding and interpretation of the administration's plan? If so, explain how your analysis differs from both viewpoints. If you agree with one of the viewpoints, explain why. If you disagree with both, formulate your own argument and address what you believe are the shortcomings of the viewpoints in the book.

Organizations to Contact

The editors have compiled the following list of organizations concerned with the issues debated in this book. The descriptions are derived from materials provided by the organizations. All have publications or information available for interested readers. The list was compiled on the date of publication of the present volume; the information provided here may change. Be aware that many organizations take several weeks or longer to respond to inquiries, so allow as much time as possible.

American Coalition for Clean Coal Electricity (ACCCE)
333 John Carlyle Street, Suite 530, Alexandria, VA 22314
(703) 684-6292
e-mail: info@cleancoalusa.org
Web site: www.cleancoalusa.org

The American Coalition for Clean Coal Electricity (ACCCE) is an organization representing the industries that work together to produce electricity via coal energy. The coalition sees coal energy as essential to the country's economy and energy security and works to develop and promote technology that will generate power from coal with near-zero carbon emissions. The ACCCE Web site's interactive map offers visitors an opportunity to explore how much power coal supplies in each state as well as the cost of power by state. News about the current state of clean coal technology is also available.

American Coalition for Ethanol (ACE)
5000 South Broadband Lane, Suite 224, Sioux Falls, SD 57108
(605) 334-3381 • fax: (605) 334-3389
Web site: www.ethanol.org

A grassroots organization representing the U.S. ethanol industry, American Coalition for Ethanol (ACE) encourages the use of plant-based fuels as an alternative to fossil fuels. The coalition presents ethanol as a clean solution to help reduce America's dependence on foreign oil and a method of improving the incomes of farmers in the United States. The guide *Ethanol Fact Book* can be downloaded from ACE's Web site along with other reports and publications about the benefits of ethanol.

American Council on Renewable Energy (ACORE)

1600 K Street NW, Suite 700, Washington, DC   20006
(202) 393-0001 • fax: (202) 393-0606
e-mail: info@acore.org
Web site: www.acore.org

The American Council on Renewable Energy (ACORE) promotes the widespread use of all forms of renewable energy in American society. This nonprofit, membership organization serves as a central voice for alternative energies including solar, wind, and biofuel. ACORE seeks to advance government energy policy toward a more sustainable future through outreach, research and publication, and the fostering of communication between industry, media, and government. ACORE's Web site contains annual reports on the status of renewable energy in America and transcripts of speeches given by organization members.

American Wind Energy Association (AWEA)

1501 M Street NW, Suite 1000, Washington, DC   20005
(202) 383-2500 • fax: (202) 383-2505
e-mail: windmail@awea.org
Web site: www.awea.org

As the trade organization of the wind industry, the American Wind Energy Association (AWEA) represents a range of organizations and individuals involved in all phases of the production of energy from wind. The association provides extensive information about the benefits of wind energy through its publications, annual conference, and education efforts in an attempt to encourage the widespread use of wind energy as an alternative to natural gas, coal, and fossil fuels. Reports, fact sheets, and other wind energy resources are available on AWEA's Web site.

Apollo Alliance

330 Townsend Street, Suite 205, San Francisco, CA 94107
(415) 371-1700 • fax: (415) 371-1707
Web site: www.apolloalliance.org

An association of labor, business, environmental, and community leaders joined together to form the Apollo Alliance following the September 11, 2001, terrorist attacks. The group seeks to advance clean energy sources in the United States in an effort to achieve energy independence. Increasing the number of green collar jobs—jobs in environmentally friendly energy-producing industries—to spur economic recovery forms the basis of the Apollo Alliance's mission. Reports and information about local branches of the organization are available on the alliance's Web site.

Edison Electric Institute (EEI)

701 Pennsylvania Avenue NW, Washington, DC 20004-2696
(202) 508-5000
e-mail: feedback@eei.org
Web site: www.eei.org

Edison Electric Institute (EEI) is a membership organization composed of U.S. shareholder-owned electric companies. EEI has eighty international electric companies that are affiliate members and nearly two hundred industry suppliers and related organizations that are associate members. It has worked since 1933 as an advocate in Washington, D.C., for legislative and regulatory policies that benefit the industry. The EEI's work focuses on specific industry issues such as electricity generation, transmission, and distribution; energy efficiency; the environment; and economics. The organization's Web site provides reports and fact sheets on alternative energy technologies such as hybrid vehicles, renewable energy, and nuclear power.

Green for All

1611 Telegraph Avenue, Suite 600, Oakland, CA   94612
(510) 663-6500
Web site: www.greenforall.org

Green for All is dedicated to creating jobs in green industries to improve the lives of Americans. The organization believes that establishing a green economy in the United States—one that focuses on industries that create clean energy—will help lift the country out of the current recession and create economic stability. Green for All's Web site provides press releases and videos touting the benefits of a green economy, information about current projects, and ways for individuals to become involved in ongoing activities.

Greenpeace USA

702 H Street NW, Washington, DC   20001
(800) 326-0959, (202) 462-1177
e-mail: info@wdc.greenpeace.org
Web site: www.greenpeace.org

For nearly forty years, Greenpeace has been working to protect and preserve the environment and its resources by raising awareness about environmental threats. Global warming and energy are of central concern to the organization. Greenpeace has laid out its solution to climate change and clean sustainable energy in the report *Energy Revolution*. The group advocates an energy policy that does not utilize coal or nuclear energy and focuses on the use of sustainable energy sources, such as solar power and wind, as the basis of emissions-free energy. The full report can be downloaded from Greenpeace's Web site along with other publications and fact sheets detailing the benefits of energy alternatives.

Institute for Energy Research (IER)

1100 H Street NW, Suite 400, Washington, DC   20005
(202) 621-2950 • fax: (202) 637-2420
Web site: www.instituteforenergyresearch.org

The Institute for Energy Research (IER) is a nonprofit organization that promotes a free market approach to energy production, research, and development. The institute believes that private industry is best suited to address the energy and environmental problems faced by the world today and that government intervention only hinders progress in finding solutions to these issues. IER contends that government policy should neither be complicated nor favor any one alternative energy technology over another. IER specifically addresses cap-and-trade policy, green jobs, and drilling for oil in America. Extensive information and reports can be accessed on IER's Web site.

Intergovernmental Panel on Climate Change (IPCC)

c/o World Meteorological Organization
7bis Avenue de la Paix, C.P. 2300, Geneva 2   CH-1211
  Switzerland
+41 227308208/54/84 • fax: +41 227308025/13
e-mail: IPCC-Sec@wmo.int
Web site: www.ipcc.ch

The Intergovernmental Panel on Climate Change (IPCC) is an international organization created through a partnership between the United Nations Environment Programme (UNEP) and the World Meteorological Organization (WMO) to assess global climate change from a scientific point of view and offer an analysis of possible environmental and socioeconomic consequences. United Nations and WMO member organizations can participate in the review of reports and plenary sessions. International assessment reports on climate change and special reports concerning issues such as carbon capture and storage are available on the IPCC's Web site.

National Biodiesel Board (NBB)

PO Box 104898, Jefferson City, MO   65110-4898
(573) 635-3893 • fax: (573) 635-7913
e-mail: info@biodiesel.org
Web site: www.biodiesel.org

The National Biodiesel Board (NBB) is the trade organization of biodiesel producers in the United States. The board seeks to establish biodiesel as an essential part of the American energy policy by 2015 and to ensure the continued growth of the industry. Information about the advantages of biodiesel fuel, quality, and sustainability is provided on the NBB's Web site. The site also provides interactive maps showing where to purchase biodiesel fuels.

National Energy Technology Laboratory (NETL)
626 Cochrans Mill Road, PO Box 10940
Pittsburgh, PA   15236-0940
(800) 553-7681 • fax: (412) 386-4604
Web site: www.netl.doe.gov

As the research and development arm of the U.S. Department of Energy, the National Energy Technology Laboratory (NETL) seeks to ensure the country's national, economic, and energy security by investigating the feasibility and benefits of implementing new energy technologies nationwide. To achieve this goal, NETL works on its own and in partnership with the private and academic sectors. The organization's key areas of focus include developing secure, reliable, and clean energy; investigating the possibility of a hydrogen economy; and increasing energy efficiency. The NETL's Web site provides access to reports on current and ongoing research.

Union of Concerned Scientists (UCS)
2 Brattle Square, Cambridge, MA   02238-9105
(617) 547-5552 • fax: (617) 864-9405
Web site: www.ucsusa.org

The Union of Concerned Scientists (UCS) is a national, non-profit organization seeking to preserve the environment and the safety of the planet by offering policy solutions backed by independent scientific research. UCS identifies global warming as a dire problem and promotes energy alternatives such as clean vehicles and renewable energy sources that would reduce the emission of harmful greenhouse gases. The organization opposes the use of nuclear power as an alternative energy supplier. The UCS's Web site contains numerous reports and analyses of alternative energy sources.

U.S. Department of Energy (DOE)
1000 Independence Avenue SW, Washington, DC   20585
(202) 586-5000 • fax: (202) 586-4403
Web site: www.energy.gov

The three-pronged mission of the U.S. Department of Energy (DOE) entails ensuring national, economic, and energy security for America; supporting technological and scientific innovation to achieve this goal; and cleaning up the environmentally harmful remains of the country's nuclear weapons complex. The DOE's research provides the basis for carrying out its mission. The agency conducts studies on climate change, nuclear physics, alternative energy supplies, and energy efficiency among other topics. The Alternative Fuels & Advanced Vehicles Data Center is a current project of the DOE; its Web site provides information about alternative fuels and vehicles. Copies of DOE reports can be found on the department's Web site.

U.S. Nuclear Regulatory Commission (NRC)
U.S. Nuclear Regulatory Commission
Washington, DC   20555-0001
(800) 368-5642 • fax: (301) 415-3716
Web site: www.nrc.gov

In 1974, Congress created the U.S. Nuclear Regulatory Commission (NRC) as an independent agency with the duty of ensuring that the country's use of nuclear power for civilian purposes is beneficial and safe for both citizens and the environment. The commission licenses, inspects, and enforces regulations on all nuclear materials, from power plants to medicine. Information about nuclear reactors and materials, radioactive waste, and nuclear security can be found on the NRC's Web site.

Bibliography of Books

Travis Bradford   *Solar Revolution: The Economic Transformation of the Global Energy Industry*. Cambridge, MA: MIT Press, 2006.

Lester R. Brown   *Plan B 3.0: Mobilizing to Save Civilization*. New York: Norton, 2008.

Michael Brune   *Coming Clean: Breaking America's Addiction to Oil and Coal*. San Francisco, CA: Sierra Club Books, 2008.

Robert Bryce   *Gusher of Lies: The Dangerous Delusions of "Energy Independence."* New York: PublicAffairs, 2008.

Helen Caldicott   *Nuclear Power Is Not the Answer*. New York: New Press, 2007.

David Craddock   *Renewable Energy Made Easy: Free Energy from Solar, Wind, Hydropower, and Other Alternative Energy Sources*. Ocala, FL: Atlantic, 2008.

Gwyneth Cravens   *Power to Save the World: The Truth About Nuclear Energy*. New York: Vintage, 2008.

Kenneth S. Deffeyes   *Beyond Oil: The View from Hubbert's Peak*. New York: Hill and Wang, 2005.

Thomas L. Friedman *Hot, Flat, and Crowded: Why We Need a Green Revolution—and How It Can Renew America.* New York: Farrar, Straus, and Giroux, 2008.

Jeff Goodell *Big Coal: The Dirty Secret Behind America's Energy Future.* Boston: Houghton Mifflin, 2006.

Jay Hakes *A Declaration of Energy Independence: How Freedom from Foreign Oil Can Improve National Security, Our Economy, and the Environment.* Hoboken, NJ: John Wiley, 2008.

Alan M. Herbst and George W. Hopley *Nuclear Energy Now: Why the Time Has Come for the World's Most Misunderstood Energy Source.* Hoboken, NJ: John Wiley & Sons, 2007.

Brian Hicks and Chris Helder *Profit from the Peak: The End of Oil and the Greatest Investment Event of the Century.* Hoboken, NJ: John Wiley & Sons, 2008.

Jay Inslee and Bracken Hendricks *Apollo's Fire: Igniting America's Clean-Energy Economy.* Washington, DC: Island Press, 2008.

Paul Kruger *Alternative Energy Resources: The Quest for Sustainable Energy.* Hoboken, NJ: John Wiley, 2006.

Fred Krupp and Miriam Horn *Earth, the Sequel: The Race to Reinvent Energy and Stop Global Warming.* New York: W.W. Norton, 2008.

Bill McKibben — *Deep Economy: The Wealth of Communities and the Durable Future.* New York: Times Books, 2007.

Susan Meredith — *Beyond Light Bulbs: Lighting the Way to Smarter Energy Management.* Austin, TX: Emerald, 2009.

Peter Newman, Timothy Beatley, and Heather Boyer — *Resilient Cities: Responding to Peak Oil and Climate Change.* Washington, DC: Island, 2009.

Greg Pahl — *Biodiesel: Growing a New Energy Economy.* 2nd ed. White River Junction, VT: Chelsea Green, 2008.

Paul Roberts — *The End of Oil: On the Edge of a Perilous New World.* Boston: Houghton Mifflin, 2004.

Christopher A. Simon — *Alternative Energy: Political, Economic, and Social Feasibility.* Lanham, MD: Rowman & Littlefield, 2006.

Richard Wolfson — *Energy, Environment, and Climate.* New York: W.W. Norton, 2008.

Index